FASHION FORECASTING

FASHION FORECASTING

Kathryn McKelvey

Reader
School of Design
Northumbria University

Janine Munslow

Head of Academic Group – Fashion
School of Design
Northumbria University

 **WILEY-BLACKWELL**

A John Wiley & Sons, Ltd., Publication

Blackwell Publishing was acquired by John Wiley & Sons in February 2007. Blackwell's publishing programme has been merged with Wiley's global Scientific, Technical, and Medical business to form Wiley-Blackwell.

Registered office
John Wiley & Sons Ltd, The Atrium, Southern Gate, Chichester, West Sussex, PO19 8SQ, United Kingdom

Editorial offices
9600 Garsington Road, Oxford, OX4 2DQ, United Kingdom
2121 State Avenue, Ames, Iowa 50014-8300, USA

For details of our global editorial offices, for customer services and for information about how to apply for permission to reuse the copyright material in this book please see our website at www.wiley.com/wiley-blackwell.

Library of Congress Cataloging-in-Publication Data
McKelvey, Kathryn.
  Fashion forecasting / Kathryn McKelvey, Janine Munslow.
      p. cm.
  Includes index.
  ISBN 978-1-4051-4004-1 (pbk. : alk. paper) 1. Clothing trade--Forecasting. 2. Fashion--Forecasting. I. Munslow, Janine. II. Title.

  TT497.M35 2008
  746.9'20112--dc22

                              2008018021

A catalogue record for this book is available from the British Library.

Typeset by Kathryn McKelvey and Janine Munslow
Printed in Singapore by Markono Print Media Pte Ltd

3 2011

Kathryn McKelvey and Janine Munslow are indebted to the following people and companies for contributing to this publication. Thanks to IN.D.EX, Sarah McDonald and Future Foundation, Melanie Marsh and Kai Chow at Here & There and Mr Doneger, of Doneger International, for permission to use the Here & There material; Fiona Jenvey CEO and Jo Little at Mudpie Design Ltd; Joyce Thornton and Sue Evans at WGSN; Christine Loyer and colleagues in the studio at Carlin International in Paris; Jaana Jätyri at Trendstop; Lucy Hailey Business Partner of Peclers Paris; Jos and John Berry at Concepts, Paris and Jennifer Kell at Concepts; Geoff and Anne at KM Associates for their help; Studio Edelkoort; Lisa Fielenbach, Product Manager at Mode Information; Klaus Vogel at WeAr Global Magazine; View Publications particularly Martin Bührmann; Ruth Capstick, graduate of BA (Hons) Fashion Marketing; Emma Jefferies for her contribution to the Design Process – Seeing.
Thanks to all for their prompt responses and permissions.
We would also like to thank Laura Armstrong, Julie Mills, Judith Bull and Sarah Kennedy for the use of their textile designs; Kristen Pickering for her help with the textile students;

Madeleine Metcalfe and Andrew Hallam, at Wiley-Blackwell, for their support, patience and input on the book.

Kathryn would like to thank Janine for her input. She would also like to thank her family for their never ending patience, lots of love to Ian, Emily, Lucy and Jack.

Janine would like to offer her sincere thanks to Kathryn and her friends and colleagues at Northumbria University, School of Design, for their support, her family Hilda, Neil, Ben, and Laurie, for their patience and Alex Rock and Leonard Le Rolland, for their much appreciated expertise and assistance.

ACKNOWLEDGEMENTS

CONTENTS

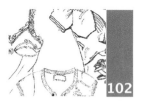

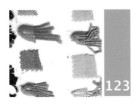
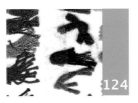

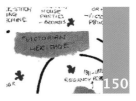

CONTENTS

This publication is designed to set out the role of forecasting in the contemporary fashion industry. The scope will be that of looking at lifestyle trends, products and services. Forecasting is a tool used by designers, manufacturers, retailers, marketers, CEOs (Chief Executive Officers) to give their brands creative dynamism in an increasingly competitive marketplace.

It is aimed at aspiring designers, intermediate students and young professionals who have some fashion knowledge and skills and professional practitioners. The book takes the point of view of the student designer who needs to interpret the intelligence, provided by the industry, in order to be self-sufficient, directional and constantly inspired. Illustrating not only how forecasting companies function – the process – the future – but also how to communicate trends using recent developments in illustration and graphics. It is an industry where 'intelligence' material is gathered, analysed and communicated to its clients as clearly, speedily and economically as possible.

A number of devices are used in this communication, primarily traditional book publishing and the Internet. Each medium has its merits, the Internet especially for speed of accessing the latest fashion information straight from the catwalk, the published book for its tactile and textural information qualities. Both approaches are essential for today's designer.

This book works in sections. The first section outlines trends and futures companies, the second a number of fashion forecasting services, those using traditional book publishing – Here & There; those appealing to a particular market, Mudpie Design Ltd (children and teenage) and Concepts Paris (lingerie); those that offer their service solely online, WGSN and Trendstop; those

well established services that offer insight such as Carlin International and Peclers, Paris.

Each company has its own approach, but they all gather fashion intelligence from around the globe that is edited and sold to their clients via subscriptions to their services.

The section also explains the flow of information which happens across a number of months in the fashion calendar.

The next 'process' section sets out to describe how to develop intelligence for a new season.
It begins by analysing the use of colour; where inspiration may be derived; fabric inspiration and the relevant trade shows – which in turn offer their own forecasting information.

Information is available everywhere, but how can more sense be made of it and how can the designer get more from a season? Part of this section deals with 'seeing' – the reading and understanding of the visual. Exercises to analyse mood boards are included to derive as much meaning and diversity as possible from a season's intelligence. This information is provided by Emma Jefferies. Emma is currently studying for a PhD in the 'visual literacy' subject area.
As consumers become more visually literate and markets more competitive this analysis offers another tool to the would-be fashion forecaster.
There are two sets of case studies in this section, one on womenswear, the other on menswear and the differences in designing for each are explored.

The final section is about layouts for publication, using typography to express mood and style and branding, and offers examples of a student's work that illustrates some of these ideas across a range of media.

FORECASTING BACKGROUND

Fashion Forecasting has emerged as an industry in line with mass production and retail development and became a serious industry after the end of the Second World War.

Changes to the fashion industry over recent history have been reflected in the manner in which prediction information is sourced, compiled and utilised.

There has been a shift from the 1960s onwards in the dominance of single fashion trends to a more pluralistic approach, mirroring the expansion of mass communication and in turn the increasing sophistication of the consumer. This has created a gradual repositioning from a marketplace that was defined by both the designer level, influencing the middle and mass market, creating designs and trends that 'trickle down' to commercial high street product and the converse effect of street styles and subcultures inspiring designers, to one which is focused on the individual and fragmented into niche markets, where the consumer's aspiration is brand led and lifestyle driven.

During the post-war period, forecasting companies compiled stories and themes each season that were easier to predict, as the market moved at a slower pace. Prediction information was compiled into books that could deliver information that was both visual and tactile. Often there was an element of hand crafting in the production.

Themes were also more predictable and often fell into evolving stories that reflected the slower moving trends of the time, for example, each season would see an update of classic stories, nautical, ethnic, purity, floral and geometric.

Typical themes from this time reflected the simplistic nature of the market, for example 'Milkmaid', 'Poacher', 'Safari', 'Country Squire' and 'Folk Story'.

Colours were more simply divided into neutrals, midtones and darks and brights and less market segmented than today. A random selection of modern theme titles reads 'Fresh Revelations', 'Allusions', 'Chameleon' and 'Filter'.

Over a period of time, wider ranging products were encompassed, sportswear, homeware and media and telecommunications and even other design disciplines, such as transportation design.

The advent of the worldwide web revolutionised the industry and enabled new Dot.Com companies to publish forecasting material that reported on global trends in a fast and distinctive manner. This required intelligence gatherers to be based in key cities across the world, reporting back any new findings; often they would be employed as freelancers or would be allied with the company's agency in that city. Many services employ illustrators and designers on a freelance basis also.

It is interesting to note that the web has changed the industry, but the tactile nature of the traditional forecasting book has still retained a market share and is essential to the fashion industry.

The traditional book is often of limited edition, for example, approximately 500 may be produced.
These books often contain fabrics from the most recent trade fairs, which have been purchased as sample lengths and hand swatched and pasted into the books. Or a combination of new and vintage fabrics may be used in the directional publications.

VIRTUAL SNO CLUB

Colour becomes full on. A group of rich saturated brights and whitened synthetic brights. For newest looks use colours in pairs with their closely toned partner or layer yellows through to reds, turquoise through green, for colour blocking on tops.

37 Phosphorous

41 Glucose

39 Static

34 Chilli

33 Cosmic

43 Juice

38 Grass

32 Moss

Mix colours through levels for placement graphics and labelling.

FINGERLESS GLOVE SWEAT

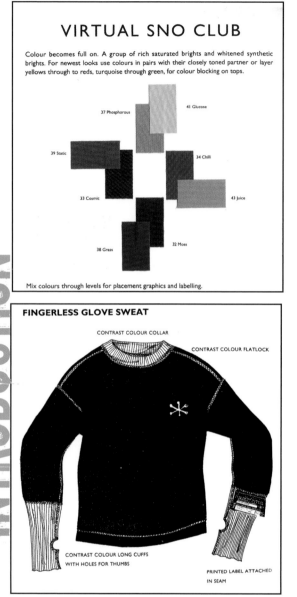

CONTRAST COLOUR COLLAR

CONTRAST COLOUR FLATLOCK

CONTRAST COLOUR LONG CUFFS
WITH HOLES FOR THUMBS

PRINTED LABEL ATTACHED
IN SEAM

The theme above illustrates a menswear active sports theme forecasting trends for Autumn/Winter 1996/97; this information would have been compiled in the spring of 1995. In examining the detail it is interesting to note how the information compares to more contemporary stories. What is striking is how forward thinking this information appears given its age.

Despite there being less focus on technology, performance related details and fabrication and the overall effect being less sophisticated and under developed than contemporary information, the general silhouette of these types of garments has only changed marginally over the lifetime of the trend to become the ubiquitous basics of the youth market.

GRAPHIC FLASHES

BADGE OR TRANSFER

SHEEN RUBBER TRANSFER PRINT

COWL NECK FLEECE PULL-OVER

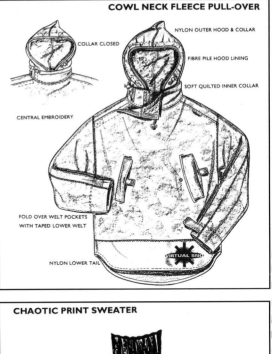

NYLON OUTER HOOD & COLLAR

COLLAR CLOSED

FIBRE PILE HOOD LINING

SOFT QUILTED INNER COLLAR

CENTRAL EMBROIDERY

FOLD OVER WELT POCKETS
WITH TAPED LOWER WELT

NYLON LOWER TAIL

VIRTUAL SNO

FOUR POCKET PULL-OVER

QUILTED ROLL-OVER SHIRT COLLAR

LARGE BACK LOGO

CONCEALED LONG
ZIP POCKETS

TIERED JACKET CUFF

CHAOTIC PRINT SWEATER

APPLIED FABRIC WITH PRINT

LABEL HANGS LOOSE FROM
RIB ATTACHMENT SEAM

The most obvious distinction, in the examples is in the graphics, which appear lacking in authenticity and complexity, however, the interaction of graphics and fashion were beginning to expand at this time so any company investing in this direction would have gained market advantage.

IMAGES COURTESY OF IN.D.EX. CIRCA 1996

03

FORECASTING AND BRAND DEVELOPMENT

As fashion consumers and products became increasingly complex in their use of information technology, materials and processes, distinct fashion brands developed identifying and marketing aesthetics, perceived authenticity and integrity to their target audience. This engenders consumer's trust in the brand's products and values and may also be perceived to qualify the taste, wealth, sub-cultural loyalty or ethical beliefs of the purchaser.

A brand is a concept that is difficult to define as it has to constantly re-invent and delineate its meaning, however it is commonly regarded as being a product and/or a service in addition to the producer or provider itself. This constant repositioning and balance of ethos and current zeitgeist provides a customer base for futures and forecasting consultancies to advise.

In many companies marketing is done by different groups, advertising, product development, consumer research, public relations, forecasting agencies can co-ordinate and focus these activities more cost-effectively and with a clear focus on being the driving force of the organisation.

Changing economic and political climates affect how brands connect with the marketplace; current reactions to issues such as globalisation, ecology, recession, terrorism, for example, create both dangers to brand perception but also opportunities, as a brand is a powerful tool for consumer reassurance, comfort through familiarity and loyalty.

Brands such as Prada, Gucci, Chanel, Hermes, Versace and Armani have immense power to generate sales in the luxury market by authorising lucrative licensed products, for example, sunglasses, luggage, perfume and jeans. A brand is the difference between a fizzy drink and 'The Real Thing'.

Modern organisations construct brand identities by appropriating a set of core values along with promoting a strong visual image, including trademarks, logos, typeface and colour. This creates a brand personality, a philosophy for consumers to aspire to. The brand's constructed image represents the essence of the organisation.

"Nothing happens until somebody brands something."

THE IMMUTABLE LAWS OF BRANDING

FUTURES CONSULTANCY
CREATIVE SOLUTIONS

The trend prediction industry becomes more diagnostic where it crosses into market research and futures consultancies, here it utilises quantitative and qualitative, mathematical and statistical techniques in order to advise brand strategies. These companies work as consultants to large companies in analysing the social trends that are affecting the consumer and advise on the best way to implement strategies within the future consumer environment across the world.

These consultancies offer insights into future consumers and how to target clients in the retail, technology, finance, automotive, food, fashion and creative industries. They build scenarios of future trends to help develop new products, or to forecast future revenue or market size. They report on emerging trends developing around the world, from the inside story on the world's most innovative cities to interviews with leading visionaries in design, architecture and consumer culture. The focus is on integrating analysis of economics, technology, politics, lifestyles, attitudes, consumption patterns and demographics.

Most businesses and other organisations know that they need to be customer focused, but may know little about their customers in reality. Futures consultancies advise that to be successful you must first understand and anticipate your customer. They provide a service for those who are looking for new ways to communicate, to develop products and strategies in a way that is more resonant and fit-for-purpose, asking how, why and where their brand needs to be in relation to current markets, and consumers' future needs. Brands can fail when they don't anticipate these shifts so this type of information is important in building

new strategies and developing company thinking on the key issues facing their organisation.

Futures consultancies work by merging trend prediction information and market research data, mixing expert interviews, intuition, quantitative and qualitative snapshots of key consumers, ethnographic and interrogative studies of target groups and by interpreting this information for specific brands to react in a more strategic and market-ready way.

There is an extensive network of professionals working in the creative and branding industries advising brands to use the most relevant and up-to-date trend information and consumer insight tools to better anticipate market needs. The aim is to help better understand the changing world; the customer's needs, both now and in the future, and the opportunities they afford.

PRODUCTS AND SERVICES:

BRAND STRATEGY PACKAGES
Can be either bespoke services or annual subscriptions, these assess performance against competition, inform on emerging trends and markets and assist in envisioning new products and opportunities using a variety of methods and techniques.

MARKET RESEARCH DATA
One of the important services offered is that of thorough market research and observations of consumer behaviour. Quantitative market research surveys are conducted, collating large-scale data; these reports enable patterns to be distinguished giving insight into the changing marketplace. In addition there are specific ethnographic and demographic studies, expert interviews, case studies and focus groups offering information on particular subjects for example, youth culture and the over 45s.

CONSUMER BEHAVIOUR

Consultancies study long-term statistical trends and provide information on emerging economic and social patterns in family life, housing, entertainment, finance and leisure activities.

METHODOLOGIES

Many consultancies have developed their own patented mapping processes or barometers using scientific methods of plotting reference points creating a more systematic approach to analysing information and synthesising the data into actionable forecasts.

CONSUMER BAROMETERS

These provide advanced planning for consumer change and aim to measure consumers concerns and confidence gleaned from long-term surveys of consumer mindsets and viewpoints.

SCENARIO BUILDING

This practice builds hypothetical situations to simulate future circumstances, anticipating future possibilities and testing probable and improbable events.

CONSUMER TYPOLOGIES

This technique creates hypothetical consumer types in order to illustrate emerging characteristics tastes and behaviour. It is useful in offering fresh approaches to existing concepts in packaging, graphics, design, manufacturing products and communications.

MACRO TREND PACKAGES

Macro packages can be aimed at outlining a number of overall global trends that are key to future business. These services would be most useful to large organisations that need to plan investments in technology and take key decisions into the medium and long-term future, for example the automobile industry.

ANTENNA

Expert opinion, intuition and insight into emerging tastes from the creative viewpoint of a global network of individual people, offers cutting edge trend analysis reporting on innovation and emerging trends from around the world. Integrating traditional and electronic approaches to the process of forecasting, this type of service is essential to those in the vanguard of fashion design, publishing and beauty.

INNOVATION – MAINTAINING THE CUTTING EDGE

In unstable markets it is difficult for businesses and their brands to retain their authenticity, integrity and vitality; these consultancies advise their clients on maintaining innovation within their organisations.

ONLINE

Directional information based resources offer detailed trend information, rigorous research and analysis of patterns in demographics, economics, technology, politics, cultural attitudes and consumer behaviour. They present daily uploads, networked from around the world, covering design, architecture, interiors, retail, product, furniture, technology, fashion and culture.

EVENTS AND BRIEFINGS

Small scale to flagship conference activities are held regularly sharing latest knowledge and insights with clients, deciphering trends to inform a wide subject area from marketing, merchandising to fashion and product design. Additionally workshops, presentations and magazines supply the 'hottest' information weekly, quarterly and biannually.

DESIGN INTELLIGENCE – FUTURES

FUTURE FOUNDATION
The Future Foundation – an international consumer consultancy.
www.futurefoundation.net

The following is an interview with Future Foundation.
The Future Foundation is an independent commercial think tank. Our work is strategic and future-focused. We advise clients on how to plan for the future by meeting developing customer needs. Our core competencies lie in understanding and forecasting social and consumer trends and analysing the extent and nature of their impact on consumer markets. Since its purchase by Experian Business Strategies in 2005, we have opened offices in France, Netherlands and Spain and continue to expand our international services.

The Future Foundation has wide experience in anticipating, understanding and forecasting changes in the way people live. Our analysis and forecasts are there to explain how the different forces – social, economic, technological, cultural and political – are shaping society, markets and the lives of individuals themselves.

Trends are systematically measured using a huge wealth of existing data and research built up over the past decade. This involves a comprehensive analysis and understanding of the present in terms of consumer attitudes and behaviour. When necessary we use primary research techniques to test and refine our propositions. Finally we aim to provide clear, action-orientated recommendations that anticipate and are in tune with future developments.

UNDERSTANDING CHANGING CONSUMER NEEDS AND BEHAVIOUR
We specialise in quantified and robust analysis of social and economic trends; clients can have confidence in our trends data as it is backed up by several years of proprietary quantitative research.
Our research is carried out twice a year and covers over 20,000 consumers across Europe and beyond. This wealth of data, trended back over many years, gives us the ability to quickly draw together comprehensive contextual data and analysis that can form a firm foundation for any project.

OUR KNOWLEDGE OF ECONOMIC TRENDS AND WIDER DATA
Our parent company Experian provides us with a wealth of further data (e.g. socio-demographic segmentation tool Mosaic, TGI, Footfall, Mori, Forrester). We also have access to top economic forecast data through our link with Business Strategies, also part of the Experian Group, who specialise in modelling the current position and future prospects of local, national and global economies in terms of employment, output, consumer spending, investment, property and asset markets.

Our relationship with Experian gives us access to unparalleled data on different economies and markets across the world at a national, regional and individual level, a unique resource for our work. It also joins us to a team of over 300 researchers, analysts and consultants across the world.

Individualism

macro trend

future foundation

TREND CARDS

FUTURE FOCUS AND FORECASTING EXPERTISE

Thanks to our understanding and monitoring of trends, we understand why consumers behave the way they do. Therefore we are uniquely placed to anticipate and forecast behaviour from current attitudes and actions.

Our nVision service contains over 500 qualitative forecasts including technology take up, spending patterns, economic indicators as well as a range of key values and attitudes. We also produce bespoke forecasts on a regular basis through our project work.

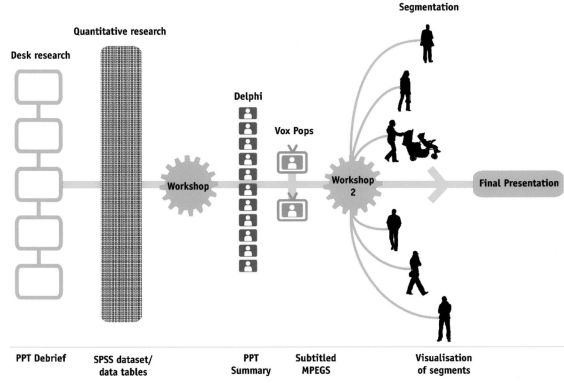

PROCESS DIAGRAM FROM FUTURE OF ENTERTAINMENT CONSORTIUM PROJECT

OUR BESPOKE DATABASE OF TRENDS 'nVISION'

nVision is our knowledge database, an online delivery of trends, research, analysis and forecasts delivered via the Internet to around 150 corporate subscribers. In addition to our proprietary research, it includes more than 120 industry, government and academic sources, including Time Use and European Social Survey. As well as providing a unique knowledge of macro trends, nVision also delivers detailed data on particular target groups, countries or commercial sectors.

CONSULTANCY

We work with 60 companies per annum, in the UK and internationally, and on ad hoc consultancy projects ranging from strategy, marketing and communications, innovation and new product development, future-proofing, forecasting, scenario planning, market mapping and thought leadership. The latter can be on specific issues or emerging trends, often providing distinctive platforms of communications activity. We use a wide range of techniques tailored to client requirements.

We take on specific consultancy briefs in areas such as forecasting, innovation and new product development, future-proofing strategy and market mapping. We also develop thought-leadership programmes on specific issues or emerging trends, often providing distinctive platforms for communications activity.

TRENDEXPRESS WORKSHOPS WITH CLIENTS

DESIGN INTELLIGENCE - FUTURES

EXTENSIVE USE OF QUANTITATIVE & QUALITATIVE RESEARCH AS A TOOL

As well as analysing our original proprietary research data from nVision, we often design original research programmes for clients covering all aspects of design, methodology, interpretation and communication of insights. We have expertise in a range of qualitative research techniques and often take an innovation approach to this type of research.

SCENARIO PLANNING FOR LONG-TERM FUTURES

Many of our clients are interested in long-term futures, generating insight which cannot always be as predictable as more medium-term forecasting and future planning. We therefore undertake scenario planning in order to help organisations imagine and plan for the future more effectively. The process highlights the principal driver of change and associated uncertainties and how they may play out in the future. We therefore present a range of possible future outcomes so that organisations anticipate, prepare for, or manage change.

MODELLING & FORECASTING

Through our own skill base and our contacts with other organisations we provide a range of powerful mathematical tools for addressing issues that are often not amenable to more traditional qualitative techniques. These include fuzzy clustering, non-linear modelling, agent-based modelling and Monte Carlo simulations. Discovering new segmentations to drive store location decisions (Woolworths), modelling household waste and electricity demands (Defra), the impact of exchange rate changes on spending by different nationalities of tourist (Historic Royal Palaces), the role and ideal pricing strategies for regional and national newspapers (Trinity Mirror) – these are just some examples of the work that we can carry out.

Recent forecasting projects include work for Listerine on the future of oral healthcare, the IPA – The future of agencies and advertising: a 10 year perspective, NS&I – 50 years of savings, Defra – The future of waste management.

VISUALISE

Another important facet of our business is our work on visualising key trends, bringing them to life in an engaging and meaningful manner. We recognise that visualisation of insight is key to their effective communication and we have developed a unique relationship with the Royal College of Art to create compelling and innovative visual communication tools.

OUR CHANGING LIVES CONFERENCE

OUR STATE OF THE NATION CONFERENCE

PHOTOGRAPHY FROM THE FUTURE OF
CANTERBURY WORKSHOP

(WITH MAPS AND VISUAL AIDS)

FORECASTING & PRODUCT DESIGN CASE STUDY – THE AUTOMOBILE INDUSTRY
Creative intelligence applied to the automobile industry.

In examining the future of any product it is imperative to define its vision of the future. Forecasting companies are employed alongside market research to build a picture of both societal changes and an understanding of how the consumer engages with the product and the brand.

TRENDS DEVELOPING FROM SOCIETAL AND TECHNOLOGICAL CHANGE

The automobile industry has to plan many years ahead and therefore commissions reports covering all aspects of social change and technology. The relevant issues for them to consider would be economics, politics, society, demographics, resources and the natural environment, mobility and spatial development information, communication and knowledge. As the automobile market is now considered mature, high growth rates can no longer be expected in Western Europe; this coupled with pressure from traffic congestion, pressure on the environment and resources have forced individual manufacturers to decide what are the most significant factors in the development of new models to them.

Research has shown that although future society would be very mobile it will also be dominated by an ageing customer base; their findings showed that the three greatest trends in future society were: increasing social disparity, greater economic insecurity and a rise in crime and breakdown of social bonds.

Challenges that they would face in the industrial environment were that competition would increase and growth will almost entirely come from emerging foreign markets. The market would consist of a number of niches.

EMOTIONAL RESPONSE TO PRODUCTS

Car and product manufacturers are increasingly carrying out research on how consumers emotionally engage with their products. In terms of automobile design, knowing how important the relationship between a car and its owner is, creates interesting design possibilities, for example, many people name their cars. It has been shown that the expression that a car's headlights and grill form affects how people relate to a vehicle. 'Somatamorphism' is the term for the human inclination to identify with objects as if they were alive.

Research has shown that some people view their cars variously as cocoons, oases of calm, thinking spaces and picnic areas reminiscent of childhood; cars generally gave people a feel good factor. The sound of a car engine was found to be comforting, people also believed that the car they buy says something about them as a person. Research also showed that these underlying influences defined niche markets. If, for example, an ageing population has buying power, this will characterise the shape, colour performance finish and interior details of the final artefact.

In applying these principles to other product areas, forecasting companies are required to understand why consumers want to identify with certain brands and their values and in which ways people relate to the products themselves

TREND ANALYSIS COMPANIES:

THE FUTURE LABORATORY
www.thefuturelaboratory.com

The Future Laboratory was established in 2001. It is recognised for its approach to trend forecasting, consumer insight and brand strategy.

The Future Laboratory have 3000 people in their 'LifeSigns Network' and have an in-house team of trend analysts and ethnographic researchers. They offer clients qualitative and quantitative insights into future consumers and how to target them. Clients in retail, technology, finance, automotive, food, fashion and creative industries have daily, weekly and quarterly news feeds, insight reports, analyses, strategy documents and brand personality audits to keep their brands on track.

FAITH POPCORN
www.faithpopcorn.com

Faith Popcorn is renowned for her trend development and books outlining lifestyle trends. She works under the name BrainReserve.

For over three decades she has provided new approaches to corporate positioning, strategic development, new products and the truth.

The company monitors the pulse of culture as it shifts and helps clients to ensure that their brand remains culturally relevant for the future by referring to the trends.

TRENDWATCHING
www.trendwatching.com

Trendwatching was established in 2002 and has its headquarters in Amsterdam, the Netherlands.

Trendwatching is an independent trend company, scanning the globe for consumer trends, insights and related business ideas. They have a network of 8,000 plus trendspotters in more than 70 countries.

Their findings are disseminated in a free, monthly trend briefing, which is sent to 160,000 plus business professionals in more than 120 countries. Their trend findings help marketers, CEOs, researchers and anyone else interested in the future of business and consumerism, to develop new products, services and experiences for and with their customers.

HENLEY CENTRE/HEADLIGHTVISION
www.hchlv.com

Henley Centre and HeadlightVision merged in 2005 to create a business with a strong base of global trends and futures insights, as well as with offices on three continents.

They are a consultancy that is led by intelligence and research. Through a combination of creativity and rigour, they 'unlock' insights through their products that shed new light on issues and empower their clients to act upon them.

Their intelligence sources offer insight into changes in consumer behaviour and motivations worldwide. They offer information in: Organising and Embedding Trends; Scenarios & Futures; Modelling & Forecasting; Future-facing Qualitative Research; Future-proofed Segmentation; and Insight-led Innovation.

This chapter illustrates some of the 'main players' in the fashion forecasting industry, how they function in any given year and what kind of services they provide to the fashion industry.

The first company, Here & There are based in New York City, USA, with most of their customers being based in the States and the Far East. As their name suggests, they gather fashion intelligence, such as designer catwalk shows, retail best sellers and street fashion from over 'There' (meaning Europe) and over 'Here' meaning the States. One of their unique selling points is the comparison they make between the designer fashion on both continents. They also report on intelligence gathered in the Far East.

Here & There work as a traditional fashion forecasting consultancy who produce publications illustrating the intelligence they create; they work in mens and womenswear. They supplement this information with a subscriber only website which highlights updates and new information as it is created. The consultancy side of the business offers 'one to one' meetings with clients, as part of their annual subscription, where clients needs are tailored to particular intelligence and forecasting material relevant to their market or niche.

A British counterpart, Mudpie Design, put much more emphasis on their website, MPD Click, which is again subscriber only, however they do not include silhouette information on the site, subscribers need to buy their publications for this lively information. The major distinction of Mudpie Design though, is that it is intelligence and forecasting aimed at companies that work in the children's to teenage markets. It uses menswear and womenswear intelligence to forecast for these younger markets. Mudpie also offer tailored consultancies to clients.

WGSN – Worth Global Style Network,

another British development, owned by Emap, however, are considered to be the world's leading global online service providing 'online research, trend analysis and news to the fashion, design and style industries'.

WGSN employ, globally, a team of 200 creative and editorial staff who work with writers, photographers, researchers, analysts and trendspotters, who gather intelligence from the latest stores, designers, brands, trends and business innovations. This is a subscription only business and there are no supplementary publications or consultancy meetings.

International companies subscribe including many fashion related industries requiring research, analysis and news, as well as emerging style trends intelligence.

WGSN truly show their global scope by having offices in New York, Hong Kong, Seoul, Los Angeles, Melbourne and Tokyo, being based in London.

Carlin, Trendstop and Peclers are more interview oriented case studies, with a 'Day in the Life' of a Trendstop Trendspotter as a feature. Trendstop is based in London, both Carlin and Peclers are based in Paris. The Carlin case study features a visit to the Paris studio.

Lucy Hailey, is a Business Partner for Peclers Paris and gives an interview about her experience in the world of fashion forecasting.

These are followed by a specialist company called Concepts who focus on lingerie trend books, presentations and consultancy.

There are a range of other major players, such as Li Edelkoort, Promostyl, Infomat, Milou Ket, Nelly Rodi, Fashion Snoops, Color Portfolio, web based Stylesight and Stylelens, Jenkins Report UK and Fashion Forecast, followed by Brandnewworld, Trendbible (interiors and homewares) and consultants and agents KM Associates.

HERE & THERE – A DIVISION OF DONEGER INTERNATIONAL

Here & There is an American fashion forecasting service based in New York City, it belongs to a larger concern: the Doneger Group. The Group is a leading American source of global market trends and merchandising strategies to the retail and fashion industry. Its network of market, trend and colour forecasting experts work together to provide clients with analysis and direction on product and business planning, they work on all stages of the design, development, and merchandising process.

All apparel and accessories markets, in retail and wholesale, men's women's and childrenswear are analysed in both Europe and the United States and key textile and trade fairs are attended and reported upon.

The Group is in a position to tailor the organisation's intelligence to address the business needs of each client individually.

The Group provide merchandising expertise through consultation with **Henry Doneger Associates** and sourcing and product development opportunities from a range of US based manufacturers and importers through HDA International.

Their trend services include **Doneger Creative Services**, the trend and forecasting division of the group covering the apparel, accessories and lifestyle markets in men's, women's and youth categories through printed publications, online content and live presentations. This division addresses the needs of retailers, manufacturers and other style related businesses.

Margit Publications provides style related trend services and fashion publications to the industry, including the Pantone for fashion and home colour system.

Tobe is an international fashion retail consulting service, best known for The Tobe Report, providing trend and business analysis to retailers in the US

But it is **Here & There** who will be explored in more detail here. They were a pioneer in the fashion intelligence industry with over thirty years of experience in trend forecasting and reporting.

Kai Chow, the creative force of Here & There, for over 23 years, in coordination with a team of in-house designers, analysts and consultants, provides colour, lifestyle, fabric and print forecasts as well as retail, catwalk, trade shows and streetwear reports. These are presented in twelve publications, eight designer collection CDs, continual online coverage, personalised consultations and resource libraries.

An annual subscription to the service provides:

FORECASTING – THE COLOR CUBICLE® – This product presents seasonal colour forecasts twice a year, two years prior to a selling season. The cubicle provides a clear, concise explanation of each colour story. It also indicates colour combinations (on the lid) and directional merchandising strategies. In the box there are yarns for designers to manipulate and make their own colour combinations.
It includes two colour cubicles – spring/summer (presented as cotton yarns) & fall/winter (presented as wool yarns), 45 colours per season, organised by family and range.

Colour cards are inserted in the Color Cubicle that explain, with mood imagery, how the stories can work in more detail.

THE COLOR CUBICLE® FALL WINTER '08-'09

here&there
WWW.HEREANDTHERE.NET

CULTURAL

SUMMER TWEED

STITCH EFFECT

FORECAST PART 1

This book includes themes, wovens, knits & prints; this is a conceptual book that forecasts lifestyle themes, fabrics and prints. It is set within the confines of approximately four themes, working with the families and ranges from the Color Cubicle®. This publication begins the creative thinking process about 17 months ahead of the season.

It includes – two publications – spring/ summer & fall/winter, a thematic overview of lifestyle and fabric; a focused outline of key fibres, yarns, wovens; knits and prints; essential colours and colour combinations, conceptual imagery with related fabric swatches; an index of publications that can be consulted for further inspiration.

FORECAST PART 2

The silhouettes book works in tandem with the Color Cubicle® and Forecast 1 to identify key silhouettes for the season. Silhouettes are presented in full length illustrations and detailed flat drawings. Also provided are trend directions for shoes, accessories and cosmetics, illustrated as drawings and photographs. It includes – two publications – spring/summer & fall/winter; a thematic silhouette overview; refined colour palette; edited fabric presentation; key items by theme; over 400 detailed flats and illustrations; thematic accessory and make-up overview.

The artwork at Here & There is created using Adobe Photoshop and Illustrator. Each theme is executed by different illustrators deliberately to bring 'a different flavour' to each theme. Each theme is usually developed from a set of four stories – look at the relationship between Romanticist – Tranquil and Juvenile, for example.

Each season is introduced by a precis 'The Season at a Glance'. This particular season works as follows:

"Observe the world. What do you see? If you look closely and listen carefully, you will notice an energising current pulsing through everyday life. A wave of consciousness washing over society, bringing together all of the elements, transforming them slowly. Our era is one of change. From the natural aesthetics of today to the technologically fuelled creations of tomorrow, the world is being reconstructed with a sense of

social and environmental responsibility. Complete with sleek modern lines, a reflection of space in its purest form. Industry and ecology are fused together in a season characterised by innovation. Hybrid building blocks integrate the essence of now with the biotechnical approach of the future. A solid foundation of eco-friendly advancements paves the way for renewal, igniting a revolution of progress. Embrace this transformation as a process that will render the past obsolete and lay the groundwork for the future."

This statement draws upon 'general' trends from a range of social, political, economic, artistic and cultural. It relates to 'lifestyle' which directly affects fashion:

"The Romanticist is a quintessential classic, blending delicate feminine elements with the tenderness of innocent youth. A 'Tranquil' sweetness is crafted from the couture, as 'Juvenile' influences leave behind the delightful air of the country. The modernist attitude reigns with a colourful burst of 'energetic' expression, smoothly materialising into 'fundamental' layers. Refinement in its highest forms. The Naturalist is a process of discovery, uncovering the history of the 'Affluent', a richly exotic and gracefully styled culture. Beneath the surface looms the mysterious 'Phantom', layered in exquisite undertones and draped in natural elegance. 'Rhythm' reconstructs casual basics in the Formalist story, while the 'Structural' side contrasts chic glamour and tailored menswear."

ROMANTICIST   MODERNIST   FORMALIST   NATURALIST

TRANQUIL   ROMANTICIST

| Babydoll Coat | Romantic Lingerie | Peasant Over Blouse | Lacy Knit | Nightgown and Petticoat |

A feminine celebration brings the inside out, the underlayer to the outerwear, in a romantically themed tale of couture-infused innocence. The once-hidden lace of lingerie appears with ruffled trims on sweetly sexy dresses. Slips and corsets are just the beginning. A foundation reminiscent of Victorian times is layered loosely and elegantly with babydoll jackets of sun-washed jacquard.

A soft blend of delicate, modern and naive influences pairs pointelle knits and crocheted cardigans. Peasant blouses take a flowing blouson shape, daintily detailed with bibs and yokes for a charming, come-hither look. A touch of classic tailoring is distinguished by hook and eye closures; lace-up ribbon ties and brassiere straps finish this tranquil love affair.

JUVENILE   ROMANTICIST

| Country Layer | Peasant Smock | Chemise Dress | Printed Fit and Flare | Naive Shirtwaist |

A little girl's dreams come to life, captured in pretty tones, whimsical prints and sweeping skirts of cotton voile, this once provincial country image takes a delightfully modern turn; a relaxed tenderness emerges. Camisoles crafted with pintucks and crocheted trim are topped with a dollop of refined yarn dye. Feminine denim implies a casual approach to romance.

Effortlessly sweet, peaceful layered smocks are the essence of this theme, overflowing with ruffles, bows and fabric-covered buttons. Pinafores are sprightly, while anything but traditional swimwear echoes the smile of a summer day. Peplum hems, puff sleeves and tiered dresses appear with every step, hinting at a soul that is light and fresh to the core.

ENERGETIC   MODERNIST

Slim and Sexy   Sporting Coat   Stretch Dress   Color Block Swim   Anorak Dressing

A colourfully dynamic attitude infuses
this story with modern flair. Bright
colours and technical materials express
a youthful image. Functionality in
design creates straight lines, smooth
and effortless. The sporting influence
actively makes its mark on the season,
jumping in with a bold approach to
colour, print and fabric. Shapes take a
mod form, materialising in mini shift

dresses and skin-tight jeans.
Playfully minimal, details are sparse as
vivid prints accent simply layered jersey
pieces, energy radiates through blouson
tops and belted tunics. High-tech parkas
invigorate the active side, while shaped
blazers pull it all together in a chic
city way. From tailored to sporty, this
energetic vision blends sexy with street
in a palette of sharp brilliance.

FUNDAMENTAL   MODERNIST

Mini Coat   Empire Tent   Couture Suit   Modest Sheath   Cropped Trench

The uptown girl steps out in a modern
city, a picture-perfect image of proper
style. Head-to-toe chic is defined by
ladylike suits in boxy shapes layered
with lightness in both colour and fabric.
Couture touches every detail, lending
a handcrafted feel. In fresh fabrics and
quaint colours, woven tops feature
saddle yokes and raglan sleeves,

exuding a feminine aura.
Free from hardware for an ultra soft
appearance, waistlines rise to empire
heights in tent dresses. Sleek. Polished.
Refined. Accessorised with sling-back
heels and tiny handbags, reminiscent
of demure sensibility, the fundamental
theme captures the metropolitan spirit
and infuses it with contemporary flair.

STRUCTURAL   FORMALIST

Slender Jacket   Belted Coat   Body and Swim   Robot Dress   Cyber Mini

The anatomy of a story reveals a need for structure, a planned combination of the casual and the formal. Heavily steeped in the masculine, a new take on old-fashioned glamour leaves behind a residue of contrast: mattes and satins stand side by side, accented by brilliant gems, corsets and bustiers are hidden beneath jackets, suggesting the sex appeal that lies just beneath the surface. Tailoring takes over, erased stripes formalise trousers and menswear takes the lead. The allure of the evening polishes the dressy side to a shine, while duller fabrics emanate a business-like aura. Suits provide stability, while shimmering details saturate this story with charisma.

RHYTHM   FORMALIST

Recycled Tunic   Revised Polo   Twofold Dresses   Urban Combo   Street Parka

A reconstruction of the classics brings a new focus to the most basic elements. Inventive and progressive, a handmade approach gives this look a dose of bright colour. Indigo weaves itself through linen, cotton, and tweed. Typographic styling sends a message of street couture. Hip, edgy and raw, this urban-inspired mixture pairs innovative seaming and colour-blocking, functionality with art, logos with numbers; drawstrings and cords perform alongside tabs, flaps and straps. At the height of creativity, recycled elements are the new shape of style: hooded dresses, oversize tops and utility pinafores. Denim is the foundation. Painted, dyed and screen-printed, topped with revised polos and woven tees, this silhouette is crafted from artistry, stitched together with the everyday casual.

AFFLUENT   NATURALIST

Exotic Shell   Statuette Suit   Bubble-over Blouse   Puff Dress   Wrapped Tunic

Richly exotic and gracefully styled,
upper echelon status has never been so
elegantly crafted. Sculpted suits stand
at the forefront of a movement defined
by charm. Sweetly puffed sleeves are
all grown up. Crowning the shoulders
of the affluent. Day gowns and night
dresses are enveloped in tradition,
steeped in antiquity, illuminated by a
sprinkling of jewels.

A glimpse at the culture celebrated
in the east and west reveals itself in
ties and bows, wrapped tunics and
silky blouses. The old world is once
again thriving, breathing life into full
skirts, dancing in jacquard dresses.
The air of well-to-do permeates each
piece, invoking a natural sense of
sophistication.

PHANTOM   NATURALIST

Tunic Knit   Sculpted Coat   Apron Dressing   Pleating Games   Simple Layer

Whispering a tale of new romance, deep
within the shadows, natural elements
assume a darker form. Layered with
exquisitely rooted undertones, pleated
with natural elegance, fluid fabrics
are the soul of this spirited story.
Discover dresses cut in asymmetric
style, voluminous cardigans billowing
in the dusk and elongated jackets
with cascading collars. Dramatically
breathtaking.

Dressing up is dressing down: mandarin
collars on simple tunic knits, sack skirts,
flowing jersey tanks, freedom is traced in
the individualistic, a transformation from
sombre reality, wrapped in an illusion-
soaked smock of delicate knit. Both
enchanting and haunting, the phantom
conjures passion, strengthening the bond
between aesthetic and attitude.

HERE & THERE

FORMALIST

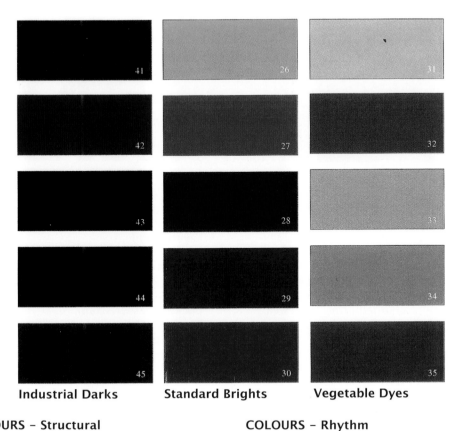

Industrial Darks   **Standard Brights**   **Vegetable Dyes**

**COLOURS – Structural
Classic Remixes**

Standard Brights with Industrial Darks
plus White.

**COLOURS – Rhythm
Casual and Basic**

Standard Brights with Vegetable Dyes
plus Indigo.

MODERNIST   NATURALIST   ROMANTICIST

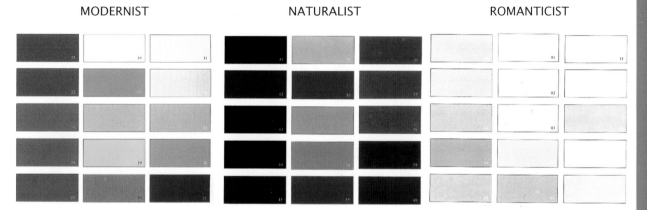

FABRICS
Natural and street

Linen – canvas. Vegetable dyed. Hemp. Raw.
Cotton – pigment vegetable. Indigo dye. Random dye.
Tweed – tropical. Handloom. Oversize plaid.
Shirting – discharged print. Menswear.
Jersey – overdye. Tie-dye. Bleached effect.
Denim – bright. Over painted. Linen.
Knits – retro stripe. Pigment coloured.

PRINTS & GRAPHICS
Urban and artistic

Typographic – numbers and messages.
Logo – street signs. Industrial logos.
Tie-dye – Japanese or African blue prints.

KEY ITEMS
Utility and street

Jackets – oversized blouson. Boxy utility. Cropped spencer.
Dresses – utility pinafore. Hooded. Layered tanks.
Tops – revised polo. Voluminous cut. Woven tees.
Tunics – fabric blocking.
Jeans – handmade jeans (hand-sewn pocket, leather strap).
Tees – overdye. Piece dye. Pigment dye. Screen prints. Raw edges.
Denim – apron skirt. Painter overall. Drainpipe jeans. Handmade.

DETAILS
Functional and homemade

Tabs and flaps.
Knit and woven blocking.
Binding and taping.
Patches and blocks.
Utility straps and flaps.
Draw cords and strings.
Hand stitching and seaming.

REVISED POLO

RECYCLED TUNIC

FABRIC BLOCKING

UTILITY SHORTS

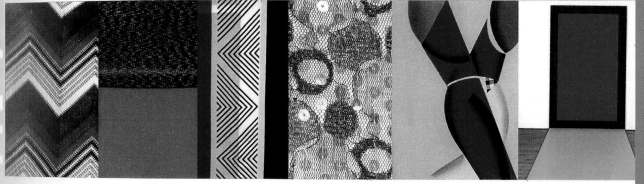

FABRICS
Industrial and sleek

Polyester – microfibre. Aesthetic and functional.
Acetate – smooth and slick.
Metal – lurex. Premium. Steel.
Viscose – silky. Fluid.
Silk – charmeuse. Printed. Satin.
Gabardine – slick. Stretch. Polyester blend. Lycra.
Jacquard – mini foulards. Geometric.
Poplin – stretch.
Shirting – menswear stripe.
Jersey – stretch. Metallic. Shine.
Denim – polyester blend.

PRINTS & GRAPHICS
Geometric and artistic

Stripe – 30s inspired. Spectator.
Geometric – de Stijl. Bauhaus inspired.
Abstract graphics.

KEY ITEMS
Tailored and stylish

Coats – belted. Elongated.
Jackets – slender.
Suits – skinny pant suits. Tight fitted.
Trousers – hot pants. Skin tight.
Cropped. High waists.
Skirts – A-line mini.
Dresses – cyber mini. Robot dresses.
Tops – assemble tanks and shells.
Geometric seaming.
Bodysuit – cut-out. Colour-blocked swimsuit.

DETAILS
Menswear and graphic

Sculpted seaming and blocking.
Oversized zipper.
Hardware trims.
Envelope pocket.
Bellow pocket.
Leather trim.
Colour-blocking.

HERE & THERE

BELLOW POCKET

FABRIC BLOCKING

BODY & SWIM

29

DROP OVERALL

HANDSEWN POCKET

HANDMADE JEAN

This spread illustrates a refined colour palette for the Formalist theme, key garment items by theme and flat drawings showing silhouette and proportion, as well as key details for the themes.

In the background there is more found imagery that helps to consolidate the theme and inspire the look.

The illustrated poses deliberately have attitude relevant to the theme. The look is quite youthful, casual, utilitarian and urban in outlook.

UTILITY JUMPER

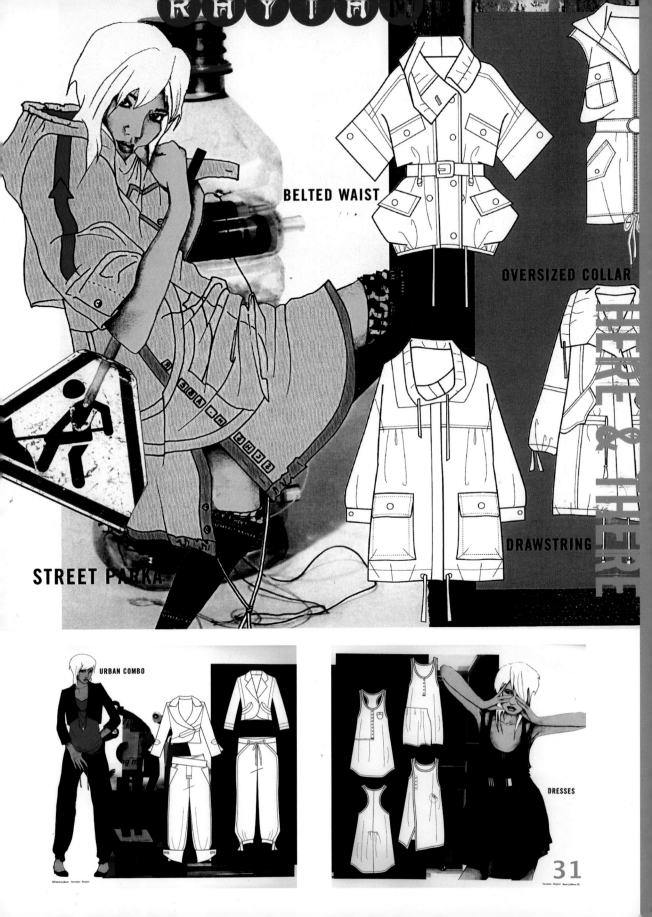

BELTED WAIST

OVERSIZED COLLAR

HERE & THERE

DRAWSTRING

STREET PARKA

URBAN COMBO

DRESSES

31

REPORTING

The Fabric Fairs – this book contains a presentation of fabric swatches, trim samples and prints from the major international yarn, textile and trim fairs. Yarns and fabrics are presented by theme, with related fashion images and updated silhouette illustrations and flats.

It includes – two publications – spring/summer & fall/winter; detailed coverage of Expofil, Pitti Filati, I-Textile, European Preview, Premiere Vision, Moda In, Prato Expo, Texworld and Asia Interstoff; swatches and photographic coverage of fabrics, yarns and trims from the leading mills; detailed information for each fabric swatch including the mill, content, width and price; revised interpretations of silhouettes from Forecast Part 2; a textile mill directory, a complete index of yarn/fabric/trim resources and their US contact.

JACKETS CLEANING UP UNIFORMS

BARCELONA

FLORENCE

BARCELONA

RETAIL DETAILS & PATTERNMAKER

This book includes photographic coverage of the retail scenes from around the world. It provides analysis of merchandise by city, colour, theme and item; sample garments are purchased, turned into specs and available for clients to borrow.

It includes – two publications – spring/summer & fall/winter; analysis of retail merchandise by city, colour and theme; focused reports of key items by merchandise category; detailed flats and specs of directional samples bought internationally; additional apparel and accessory images available on request.

FLORENCE

MILAN

BARCELONA

PATTERNMAKER JACKET – OFFBEAT MILITARY

ITEM Offbeat military jacket by/from Cat's - Seoul.
SIZE M.
FABRIC 100% Cotton.
COLOR Khaki.
DETAIL Multi-colored buttons. Lace-up sleeves. Back belt.
REFERENCE #7061.

Body Width: 1" below armhole	18"
C.F. Length	23 1/2"
Shoulder Width	14"
Shoulder Seam Width	4"
Bottom Width	24"
Armhole Front	10 1/2"
Armhole Back	10 1/2"
Sleeve Length	25 1/4"
Cuff Height	3 3/4"
Cuff Width	5"
Horizontal Back Neck Width	7 1/4"
Neck Drop Front	4 1/2"
Neck Drop Back	1/2"
Collar Height (C.B.)	1 7/8"
Collar Stand	1 5/8"
Collar Point	3 1/4"
Side Seam Length	18"

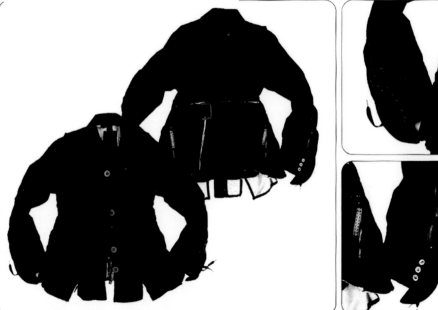

BARCELONA

FLORENCE

FLORENCE

NEW YORK

here & there

John Galliano

0 to 10 of 1

here & there ⏮ ▶ ❚❚ ⏭

40 to 50 of 9

here & there ⏮ ▶ ❚❚ ⏭
Print

DESIGNER COLLECTIONS CDs
These cover the New York, London,
Milan and Paris runway collections.
The CDs are categorised by designer,
merchandise classification, accessory,
colour, print and fabrication. Each CD
contains digital presentations identifying
the key trends for the season.
They include – eight designer collections
CDs – spring/summer & fall/winter;
complete coverage of over 300 designer
lines; photographic and written
analysis of the collections by theme,
merchandise category, colour, print,
fabric and accessory; images in JPEG

20

34   comme des garcons

Soon Ju Kam

Central Saint Martin

here(&)there®

Print

esigners

format for use in presentations and layouts. American & European Collections Compared – this book presents both sets of collections, juxtaposed to compare their similarities and differences by theme and trend. It includes – two publications – spring/summer & fall/winter; photographic coverage of the New York, Los Angeles, London, Milan and Paris collections: analysis of the women's and men's collections by theme and trend.

HERE & THERE

Tao – Paris

Vuitton – Paris

Rocha – London

Vuitton

Vuitton – Paris

Vuitton – Paris

Vuitton

STREETWEAR & RESORT
This book presents the summer resort and street fashions of St Tropez, Paris, London, New York, Los Angeles, Milan, Sao Paulo and Sydney. It also includes coverage and analysis of the spring/summer menswear collections in Milan and Paris.
It includes – one summer publication; photographic coverage of resort and street fashions; photographic coverage and analysis of the spring/summer menswear collections; detailed flats and specs of directional samples bought internationally.

Rucci – New York

Bartley – New York

Scott – New York

Lepore – New York

Y3 by Yohji Yamamoto – New York

Proenza Schouler – New York

Shops & Spots – lists boutiques, shops, retailers and mass merchants in the US, Europe and Asia.
Directional boutiques are located by neighbourhood on detailed city maps. Store openings and closings are updated on the website.
It includes – city by city shopping guides of New York, Los Angeles, London, Paris, Milan, Florence, Rome, Barcelona, Amsterdam, Antwerp, Dusseldorf, Cologne and Tokyo; over 5,600 listings of boutiques, shops, retailers and merchants; shops 'not to miss' in each neighbourhood.

ONLINE TREND REPORTING

This includes – photographic coverage of the designer collections; retail and streetwear photographs; detailed reports from international fabric and print shows; special features with news from specific market sectors; city by city shopping directory and maps; textile mill directory, a complete index of yarn/fabric/trim resources.

STUDIO SUPPORT

Personalised Consultations – cater to client's specific needs. Some areas of consultation include overview of trends as they relate to specific markets and product lines; customised colour, fabric and print directions; strategies for updating key items and best sellers.
Also:
In-house Presentations.

Fabrics, Yarns, Prints, Colours (with over thirty years of colour and yarn swatches). Garment Samples.

WEB SUPPORT
Retail Updates.
Designer Collections Coverage.
Trade Show Reports.
Streetwear Reports.
Shops & Spots Directory.
Textile Resource Directory.

registered user login

Email address

If you're not registered
click here

Login

⊞ lightbox ?

There are currently 0 items in your lightbox.
View contents

quick links

welcome

A subscription to mpdclick.com is the ultimate desktop intelligence resource to keep you informed of rapidly changing fashion and consumer trends.

➡ demo
➡ free trial
➡ whats new ?

move your point and select an area of interest

MUDPIE DESIGN LTD
Background

Mudpie Design Ltd, founded by Fiona Jenvey, CEO, brings together an international team of designers and trend analysts working on youth directions and apparel. The Mudpie Design network spans 50 countries, including a large graphic and textile design consultancy based in the UK.

Mudpie Design Ltd was started 15 years ago as a design consultancy aimed at addressing the design needs of large retailers and suppliers who needed intelligence for their teenage, youth, street, tween and childrenswear markets. Mudpie is unique in that it specialises in this area, whereas most other trend consultants are womenswear focused. This has proved to be a successful strategy for Mudpie's consultancy, trend book publications and their online service

www.mpdclick.com, which all focus strongly on these younger areas.

Mudpie also work with 'fashion forward' mens and womenswear brands who 'borrow trends' from teen and youth fashion, something that they often see happening on the international runway with designers Agatha Ruiz de la Prada, JC de Castelbajac, House of Holland, and Eley Kishimoto. This enables Mudpie to relate their business to a very wide client base which can then be serviced via a bespoke consultancy service, a printed trend book or via daily online updates on mpdclick.com.
This in itself responds to the needs of the customer by offering a highly relevant service, delivered in the customers preferred format, at the exact time that they need it. Mudpie's design and trend studio operates at a very fast pace ensuring the main teen and youth areas change quickly to reflect the latest music, technology and street scenes.

Welcome back
Kathryn, you are logged in.
My account
Log out

⊞ lightbox ?

There are currently 15 items in your lightbox.
View contents

You currently have previously registered trend books.

Register a book

About this book

Previous seasons

Buy this book

Register your book

Technical support

40

colour source autumn / winter 0809

cotton inc
mudpie
pantone

			17-1464 TC		19-1533 TC
11-0607 TC	14-0000 TC	11-0710 TC	16-3911 TC		11-4301 TC
13-0915 TC			19-3716 TC	17-1534 TC	12-4305 TC
15-1220 TC	17-0636 TC	14-0755 TC	19-1761 TC	18-3415 TC	
16-1432 TC			18-1756 TC	17-3802 TC	15-1315 TC	19-4044 TC
17-1128 TC	15-0538 TC	14-0647 TC	19-1850 TC	19-3230 TC	13-1114 TC
	13-0650 TC		18-2328 TC		14-1418 TC	18-4834 TC
19-1317 TC		15-1054 TPX		19-2428 TC		19-4006 TC
				19-2524 TC	13-1106 TC	

a diverse palette full of intrigue
calm cool neutrals tame an orchestra of opulent hues
honing a playful yet classic arrangement

fetish du jour

Let yourself be carried away by eroticism, learn to enjoy without regrets. Voluptuous looks, subtly excessive, embodying carnal and organic luxury.

Colours pull at the weary mind. Blue and brown lead in all directions. Brown leads to rust or wood or chocolate. Blue leads to metal or plastic or the sky.

Pantone 11-0602 tc   Snow white
Pantone 15-3825 tc   Lavender Lustre
Pantone 19-3964 tc   Mazarine Blue
Pantone 19-3906 tc   Dark Shadow
Pantone 19-1522 tc   Zinfandel
Pantone 19-1215 tc   Sesame
Pantone 19-1314 tc   Bracken

MUDPIE DESIGNED

Staff are encouraged to attend cultural events including music festivals, street events, art and design exhibitions and the seasonal trade and fashion shows.

Fiona Jenvey is a creative designer and analytical thinker, with an extensive knowledge of global lifestyle trends. Fiona presents her trend forecasts to audiences in London, New York, Copenhagen, Amsterdam, Barcelona and Hong Kong. Her seminars offer information based on the Mudpie brand's five seasonal children's and youth trend books and their online service mpdclick.com.
The company has an exhibition stand at Premiere Vision in Paris and welcomes international visitors.

TRENDS
Colour and style predictions are formulated using analysis of current and emerging fashion product and lifestyle trends.
They provide focused collages of relevant imagery, directional graphics and Pantone® referenced colour palettes. These are designed for use alongside their mini reports, compiled using information gathered from trade fairs and a wide range of retail sources, to create instant trend presentations for colleagues or customers.
They give designers downloadable trend-led graphics and prints available in vector formats.

N ITS DISORDER CHAOS

MUDPIE DESIGN LTD

TREND BOOKS

Their five trend, graphic and colour forecasting books provide customers with hundreds of inspirational garment and accessory styles, prints and graphics. Each book is packaged with a Pantone® referenced colour card, fully vectorised artwork on DVD and regular online updates.

Their trend forecasting books provide design solutions for all areas of the children's market from babies through to teens plus young adults.

These trend publications are created by a collaborative team of fashion analysts, who work on mpdclick and for their design consultancy.

They follow the traditional publishing schedule, two seasonal collections a year, but they appreciate that trend information is constantly evolving, so they continue to monitor the markets, after publication, and add online trend updates throughout the season.

BOOKS – MPK FEMALE
Female trends – styling, graphics
and prints based on trend-led colour
palettes.
Fashion trends, arranged into complete
wardrobes, which can be lifted straight
from the book or easily modified to suit
client's exact requirements.

MPK MALE
Male trends – active teenagers and
young men styling, original graphics,
eclectic garment ranges that reflect
sport, urban street and popular culture.

mudpie

43

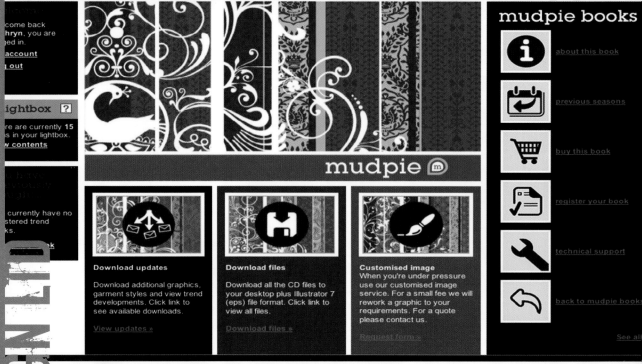

mudpie ⓜ

ⓘ

Download updates

Download additional graphics,
garment styles and view trend
developments. Click link to
see available downloads.

View updates »

Download files

Download all the CD files to
your desktop plus Illustrator 7
(eps) file format. Click link to
view all files.

Download files »

Customised image
When you're under pressure
use our customised image
service. For a small fee we will
rework a graphic to your
requirements. For a quote
please contact us.

Request form»

See all

MUDPIE DESIGN LTD

pantone - ss09 -
fetish dujour
09/10/2007

cotton inc
blurred exi
04/10/2007

otton
tuitiv
/10/20

-
ism

CUTIPIE
Layette trends – garment styles, naïve
graphics and functional accessories.
Eight trend based collections have a
story which translates straight to retail
ranges or can be adapted easily to
individual requirements.

MINIPIE
Kids trends – this book is a mix of
silhouettes, prints and motifs.
Commercial trend and colour forecasting
underpins this seasonal library. It is
packaged to make range formulation,
garment design and graphic or print
application straightforward.

MUDPIE
Tween and junior trends – designs
created for the fashion conscious
tweens: girls and boys who want to
be grown up and establish their own
personal style.
Mudpie identify with kids and the pre-
teen world through analysis of lifestyle
and cultural influences, giving this
forecasting tool the lead in targeted
design for this area of the marketplace.

ic - ss09 -
sion
7

lenzing - s/s 09 -
aquatic
17/09/2007

lenzing - s/s 09 -
harvest
17/09/2007

lenzing - s/s 09 -
posh
17/09/2007

lenzing
repose
17/09/20

female

03/10/2007

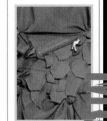

RUNWAY

Each season international designers launch their collections of new garments and accessories at the fashion weeks and design shows.

With increasing demand for 'fast fashion' companies convert the latest runway trends into retail ranges within a six week period.

Within days of the catwalk shows, thousands of runway images are sorted into the designers' photo galleries on mpdclick. They are tagged according to season, show and designer for ease of searching. They also provide a breakdown of the key shapes, details and trends which embody the designer's signature styles – plus seasonal overviews, previews and highlights.

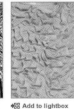

art and design focus - art deco
09/05/2007

art and design focus - art nouveau
09/05/2007

art and design focus - cubism
09/05/2007

art and design focus - expressionism
09/05/2007

art and design focus - futurism
09/05/2007

culture reports

technology

Search this section.

art and design focus - impressionism
09/05/2007

art and design focus - op art
09/05/2007

art and design focus
09/05/2007

03/10/2007

alism

no place like home - alternative living spaces
12/10/2007

aerogel - a miracle material ?
19/09/2007

technology trends, september 2007
05/09/2007

wearable technology - august 07
28/08/2007

brand new ispo - munich (ger) - ss/08 - unisex
17/07/2007

technology trends - june 07
31/05/2007

technology report - anterior insight - march 07
12/03/2007

techno tots - anterior insight - february 07
11/02/2007

⊕▒ Add to lightbox
© flickr.com

⊕▒ Add to lightbox
© flickr.com

⊕▒ In lightbox
© flickr.com

⊕▒ In lightbox
© flickr.com

⊕▒ In lightbox
© flickr.com

ior design

Add to lightbox
steez

⊕▒ Add to lightbox
madsteez

⊕▒ Add t
madstee

⊕ Add t
adsteez

CULTURE

Clothes designers, fashion stylists, illustrators and graphic designers take inspiration from lifestyle trends, street and urban culture, music, merchandise and a wide variety of art. Mpdclick trend spot at music festivals and create photographic reports about art & design exhibitions – from graffiti shows to fine art.

Thousands of photographs are posted on the site each week, customers can browse and save their favourite images to their personalised 'lightbox' which allows them to keep all items of interest in a downloadable folder.

paris vintage (fra) -
june 07 - male
13/07/2007

london - vintage -
june 07 - male
05/06/2007

male vintage -
london (gbr) -

vintage accessories
- london (gbr) -

Add to lightbox
411

Add to lightbox
agent sparks

Add to lightbox
olde english

Add to lightbox
boost

Add to lightbox
xbox360

See more pictures

london

skate and ski

Add to lightbox
pop cling

Add to lightbox
wallin

Add to lightbox
amada

Add to lightbox
salomon

Add to lightbox
ac/dc

See more pictures

back to city guides

west end

knights-
bridge

camden

shoreditch

online
coming soon

shopping key		
$ budget prices		accessories
$$ middle high street prices		footwear
$$$ top high street prices		boutique
$$$$ designer prices		market
flagship store		chain store

Add to lightbox
eez

Add to lightbox
madsteez

Add to lightbox
madsteez

d to lightb
eez

d to lightb
eez

http://www.madsteez.com/heydiksnike.htm

RETAIL

They visit fashion centres worldwide to take pictures of displays in store windows and the fashion, fabrics, home-ware, toys and displays inside them.

The client has the option to view their retail intelligence reports by city or garment types, vintage or sport areas which are categorised by age and gender for ease of browsing.

There are thousands of images to download from a diverse range of reports, including T-shirt graphics, most unusual denim details and latest accessories. All compiled to give an insight into what's 'hot' on the high street and a universal grasp of emerging trends.

MUDPIE DESIGNED

+🔳 Add to lightbox
michele lemaine pour tissus

+🔳 Add to lightbox
monteoliveto

+🔳 Add to lightbox
nephila tessuti

+🔳 Add to lightbox
nephila tessuti

+🔳 Add to lightbox
michele lemaine pour tissus

- Tactile surface designs saw a definite move towards a textured surface
- Printed fabrics are creased, while knits are creased before being coated with metallic, with the uncoated creases creating contrasting creases through the coat as the fabric relaxes back to its natural state
- Dramatic devoré effects create interesting 3d patterns

sportswear - s/s 07 - new style rubber
16/05/2007

sportswear - s/s 07 - skate of the art footwear
09/05/2007

alexander mcqueen for puma - s/s 07
18/04/2007

urban sportswear - female - a/w 07/08
18/04/2007

sportswear - a/w 08/09 - yohji yamamoto meets adidas - female
16/04/2007

sportswear - s/s 07 - yohji yamamoto meets adidas - female
16/04/2007

sportswear - s/s 08 - performance - female
13/04/2007

sportswear - body form
11/04/2007

sportswear - s/s 08 - its all in the bag
11/04/2007

luxury - sportswear -

TRADE FAIRS

Short lead times and reduced travel budgets have made it increasingly difficult for buyers and designers to visit the major international trade fairs and analyse key trends. Mpdclick attend these events for their subscribers and post photo reports and picture albums online on return.

They cover fashion, sports and fabric, as well as design and lifestyle shows, providing focused interpretation of the dominant styles for all market groups, from baby to young adults.

Future dates and press releases for all the trade events covered are provided online to help customers to plan their diaries.

mpdclick

trends

flash trends

overviews

celebrity style

beauty

features

← back

press 'esc' to exit full screen

main menu
free trial

MUDPIE DESIGN LTD

CONSULTANCY

Mudpie offer the full design process from presentations, trend boards and colour direction to final graphic and garment ranges as a bespoke consultancy service.
They will undertake small, one off projects, to full outsourced solutions.

They have developed a library of thousands of garment shapes and styles which they update to meet the needs of consultancy customers, to assist them in developing their garment ranges.

They have experience of working with manufacturers around the world from the trend and design process through to fabric selection, sampling and final range presentation.

Their knowledge of the processes employed in vertical garment manufacture gives them the expertise to offer a commercial design solution.

Fiona Jenvey sits on various international colour panels and has access to colour information from Pantone and Cotton Inc.
Mudpie's colour analysis is not just theoretical, they interpret overall colour trends into ranges of colours for individual companies and countries, depending on many different factors, for example, the demographic of their customer base. They can present this information as formal presentations, or in board or document form.

WGSN (WORTH GLOBAL STYLE NETWORK) part of the EMAP Group based in London.
www.wgsn.com

WGSN is the world's leading online trend analysis service, it has been established since around 1998. They provide creative and business intelligence for fashion, apparel, style and retail businesses across the world.
Their team of editors, designers, stylists and trendspotters have industrial experience from brands that include Tommy Hilfiger, Wrangler and Top Shop. They travel the globe to deliver a 360° view of the fashion and retail industries – all focused on providing subscribers with 'need-to-know' information that will deliver value to their business.

A subscription to WGSN provides:

TRACKING FUTURE DIRECTIONS
In-depth analysis providing future intelligence (24 months ahead).
Forward trend tracking (12 months ahead).
Close-to-season overview (3-6 months ahead).

EXTENSIVE COVERAGE
Catwalk shows: major and emerging international shows, including thousands of catwalk photographs
140 tradeshows per year
Street reports from around the world
In-depth retail reporting
Store windows: global coverage, photographs and analysis
Downloadable sketches and graphics
Photo and image libraries for womenswear, menswear, childrenswear, intimate and swimwear, denim, youth/junior, active sports, accessories, footwear, interiors and materials.

The WGSN-edu site allows free access to the WGSN website to students and academic staff all over the world; those studying fashion, textiles, design and related fields are able to use 'time delayed WGSN content to further their knowledge of the industry and help with their studies. Student specific content is created within the 'Student Magazine' and 'Careers Advice'. These include interviews with the cutting-edge players in fashion, young designers, successful recent graduates, design and style innovators. Also words of advice from established names on how to 'make it', plus features on student issues around the world, questions and answers, college life, research round-ups and college style reports.

The professional WGSN site consists of 16 Directories which are accessible through 'global' navigation at the top of the page. Each Directory consists of 'local' navigation on the left hand side of the page where more in-depth information, regarding that Directory, is found.
The Directories are:
NEWS, BUSINESS RESOURCE, TRADE SHOWS, MATERIALS, CATWALKS, THE MAGAZINE, THINK TANK, TRENDS, WHAT'S IN STORE, RETAIL TALK, CITY BY CITY, BEAUTY, YOUTH/JUNIOR, ACTIVE SPORTS, GRAPHICS and GENERATION NOW.

LOG ON ●
MY WGSN ●
MY SCRAPBOOK ●
CALENDAR ●
PLAN AHEAD ●
CONTACT US ●
FAQS ●
ASK WGSN ●
ABOUT WGSN ●
SITE MAP ●
WGSN SEMINARS ●
CAREERS ●

WGSN LOGO & LOG-IN

WGSN LOGO

WGSN

LOG-ON FOR
SUBSCRIBERS

GLOBAL NAVIGATION
–THE DIRECTORIES

SEARCH
FUNCTIONS

SCROLL BAR

LOCAL
NAVIGATION

LATEST NEWS
UPDATES

LATEST IN EACH
DIRECTORY

QUICK LINKS

US LIFESTYLE MONITOR

The Directories are always visible, each home page has local navigation also and information is accessed through clicking on the 'thumbnails' on each page, or on the underlined text.

There are 'archives' as well as each Directory of information. The site is a very deep and rich resource.

WGSN HOME PAGE

ANATOMY OF A WEBSITE

MATERIALS

This Directory is aimed at designers and suppliers; it contains information on fibres, yarns, textiles and materials as the basis of product development for the apparel, home furnishing or interiors sectors. It also provides the latest technological developments.

TEXTILE NEWS TODAY offers updates on the major events affecting the global textiles industry.

TRADE SHOWS offers coverage of the major yarn and fabric shows for apparel and interiors. It includes Events & Trade Show News with views and previews of trade shows, events and conferences.

SWATCH REPORTS provide selected seasonal fabrics from international textile manufacturers including source and fabric details.

TRENDS RESEARCH links to the seasonal early trend research on colour, materials, knit, textiles and graphics.

INNOVATION offers news and features on the latest innovations in the textiles industry, focusing on 'smart' clothing, new materials and nanotechnology.

DENIM links to the denim directory, highlighting textile developments, washes, trims, labelling and styling directions.

COTTON MONITOR links to the collaboration with Cotton Incorporated outlined in the Business Resource Directory.

GLOSSARY offers a comprehensive alphabetical list of fibre, yarn, fabric and non-apparel materials terms and definitions.

Materials has Calendar, Scrapbook, Archive and Search functionality.

CATWALKS

This Directory is aimed at buyers and designers. It contains all of the 'hottest' looks for commercial development.

IMAGES contains full photographic coverage of menswear, womenswear, haute couture and accessories. All of the leading shows are recorded plus 'up and coming' designers. The photographs are made available within hours of each show taking place.

DAILY BUZZ offers daily reports by WGSN fashion journalists direct from Milan, Paris, New York and London.

STYLEFILE offers a weekly analysis of the key directions to emerge from each of the major runway schedules.

OVERVIEWS offers an in-depth analysis of the latest trends including key looks, silhouettes, colour, fabrics, print, pattern and knit.

KEY ITEMS ANALYSIS offers detailed commercial analysis by product type.

Catwalks has Scrapbook, Calendar and Archive functionality but with the addition of a Photo Search which offers tagged photos indicating category, product type and colour/fabric. It also offers Zoom, a tool allowing the user to magnify design elements, such as embroidery, stitch detail, print, pattern or buttons.

© WGSN 2007

WGSN

Preen   Giambattista Valli   Louis Vuitton   Helmut Lang

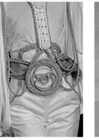
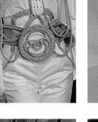

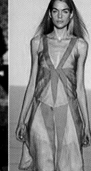

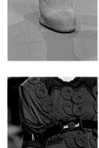

Dolce & Gabbana   Dolce & Gabbana   Rue du Mail   Valentino

NEWS

This Directory is aimed at all personnel from designers and merchandisers to CEOs. It reports on the key events from around the world as they happen, rapidly breaking and monitoring the news with a speed that the printed press cannot match.

DAILY NEWS includes the latest company results, what's happening in the stock markets, newly appointed head designers at which labels, the catwalk shows that have captured the zeitgeist, who has lost a CEO and who has found one.

GLOBAL NEWS features daily stories organised by region to target relevant information.

IN THE MARKETS has daily updates and share price movements affected by events in the news. In terms of 'functionality' there is access to '10 Day News' to rapidly catch up on news missed whilst on vacation.

An Archive provides access to News from previous days, months and years. There is a Search by 'date' and 'keyword' facility also.

Scrapbook allows users to file articles and archive selected reports for easy reference and project grouping.

BUSINESS RESOURCE

This Directory contains information targeted at CEOs.

MARKET RESEARCH contains executive summaries from Mintel, Verdict Research, Euromonitor International, Packaged Facts and others. It provides insight and forecasts covering the 'major players' and key trends.

LEADING RETAILERS ranking the world's biggest retailers by annual sales.

STRATEGY TALK challenges opinion-led features and interviews.

REGIONAL FOCUS offers news, information, forecasts and statistics archived by region such as, China, Japan, India, North America, Asia, Europe, Australasia, Africa and the Middle East.

GLOBAL SOURCING GUIDE offers country profile guides covering news, production, employment, exports, competitive benefits, case studies and links to other useful websites.

US LIFESTYLE MONITOR features a collaboration between WGSN and Cotton Incorporated, based on Cotton Incs. Lifestyle Monitor research programme, which records America's attitudes towards apparel and home furnishings.

ADDITIONAL BUSINESS TOOLS – Useful Links – offers information on key tariffs and quotas providers and Ideas Bank makes the connection between concept development and business.

Business Resource has Scrapbook, Archive and Search functionality.

TRADE SHOWS

This Directory is aimed at designers and buyers. This coverage of the world's major trade events provides subscribers with the first indications of a coming season by using product focused photo reports highlighting the 'hottest' looks and brands.

Eighty major US, European and Asian textile and apparel fairs are covered including: Première Vision, Pitti Immagine Uomo, CPH Vision, Magic, Project, Tranoi, Ispo, Mode Enfantine, Lingerie Paris, Action Sports Retailer, GlobalShop, Interstoff Asia and BREAD & Butter.

Interiors, footwear and leather fairs are also covered: Maison & Objet, Heimtextil, Milan Furniture Fair, Asia Pacific Leather Fair, Micam and Premiere Classe.

NEWS offers reports direct from the shows.

REPORTS offers photo reports published within six days of the shows closing including detailed trend analysis.

SECTOR SPECIFIC LINKS provides a rapid way of viewing the latest reports in each product category.

REPORT TIMETABLE offers an 'at a glance' list of the trade shows that WGSN will cover each season with publication dates and links to the live report.

Trade Shows has Scrapbook, Archive and Search functionality with a 'Calendar' guide to trade events worldwide.

THE MAGAZINE

This Directory is aimed at anyone connected with fashion, media and marketing who wants to access new media and advertising trends.

FEATURES contains reports on 'tastemakers' in art, media and culture; reviews of books, new magazines and film trends, marketing and lifestyle influences.

AD CAMPAIGN TRENDS offers a twice yearly analysis of fashion brand and designer advertising campaigns, assessing trends in film and art direction and photography, models and locations.

MEDIA NEWS offers news from the media and marketing.

TOP 10 NEW AD CAMPAIGNS offers creative advertisements from television, cinema, press, poster and viral ads from across all categories of the style and design industries in Europe, US, Asia and major markets worldwide.

CELEBRITY STYLE offers photo coverage of the Oscars and Golden Globe red carpet awards ceremonies. Celebrities and local trendsetters are covered from Asia, Europe and the Americas.

GOSSIP offers celebrity news.

FASHION WEEKS offers information about new designers emerging excluding Milan, Paris, New York and London which are covered in Catwalks.

THE PR LIST offers a contact list of the top public relations companies, their strengths and whom they represent.

EDITOR'S CHOICE offers a summary of the most influential stories of the month.

The Magazine has Scrapbook, Archive and Search functionality.

THINK TANK

This Directory is aimed at brand directors, marketers and CEOs.

It intends to anticipate the future, to think about the 'why' and 'how' behind long-term trends.

The scope of the Directory is advertising, architecture, media, lifestyle, work, health, entertainment, travel, sport, science and technology, food and drink and automotive design.

CONSUMER ATTITUDES offers the changing thoughts and feelings of the consumer. Consumer trends, based on the study of international media, demographic analysis, feedback from WGSN's global correspondents and industry specialist interviews are 'summed' up.

IDEAS BANK offers interviews and commentary from trend researchers and industry specialists. It tracks future concepts and products across a range of industries and links them to consumer attitudes.

PHOTOFILE offers inspiration from around the globe including research photographs of places, spaces and other inspiration.

SEASONAL RESEARCH offers highlights of the new season's directions that will influence product development: colour, materials, graphics, yarn, textiles and knit. New cultural drivers such as influential art and design exhibitions, films, new books and social moods are tracked.

Facehunter

Beard balaclava on kitsunenoir.com

TRENDS

This Directory is aimed at designers, buyers, merchandisers and marketers. It intends to allow the professionals to plan, design and think ahead.

EARLY RESEARCH offers key moods, cultural indicators and long-term trends that will affect style related businesses. Influences and cultural moods are tracked to find the new and innovative, from international art and design exhibitions, films and new books to cities and underground trends that reflect the zeitgeist.

PRODUCT DIRECTIONS offers sector and product specific information developed from early trend research. Each sector has informative design packs highlighting colour, key items for the season, research influences, textiles and styling.

- **Womenswear:** directions designed to inspire and inform on colour, fabrics and styling.
- **Menswear:** themes, styling directions, colour statements and fabrications.
- **Intimate apparel/swimwear:** colour, pattern, styling and trims for these specialist sectors, including direction for men's and womenswear.
- **Kidswear:** directions including print, graphics and styling for girls, boys and babies/toddlers.
- **Footwear:** women's, men's and sports styling, shapes, materials and technical innovation.
- **Accessories:** rapidly changing sector focuses on bags, belts, leather goods, jewellery, eyewear and watches.
- **Denim:** textile developments, washes, trims, labelling and styling directions.
- **Colour:** from concept to commercial reality.
- **Interiors:** home trends – key product categories including bed and bath linen, tabletop and promotional gifts.

FAST TRACKS offers a continual feed of real-time fast response information, confirming or updating trends.

Trends has Scrapbook, Archive and Search functionality.

TRENDS SEASONAL RESEARCH

SPRING / SUMMER 2009

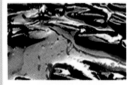

SURFACE

17.07.07

EARLY RESEARCH

07.08.07

TEXTILES

24.08.07

EARLY COLOUR

29.06.07

KNIT

24.08.07

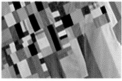

GRAPHICS

31.08.07

COLOUR PALETTES

Butterfly
Indian-inspired culottes - circular-cut leg___

neutrals

ALMOND	WHITE	DOVE	ELEPHANT	CACTUS	BONE
pantone ® 13-0607	pantone ® 11-0601	pantone ® 15-4502	pantone ® 16-1107	pantone ® 16-0713	pantone ® 13-0513

orange/reds

VANILLA	PLANTAIN	ELASTOPLAST	CORAL	TOMATO	DESERT FLOWER
pantone ® 12-0713	pantone ® 12-0822	pantone ® 13-1023	pantone ® 17-1547	pantone ® 18-1445	pantone ® 16-1529

pinks

ALABASTER	FRESCO	RED EARTH	PLUM	SORBET	CANDY FLOSS	JELLY
pantone ® 11-0603	pantone ® 13-1512	pantone ® 16-1516	pantone ® 18-1616	pantone ® 17-1929	pantone ® 13-2806	pantone ® 17-1753

browns

BISCUIT	TEA	CARAMAC	GROUNDNUT	COFFEE	COPPER LUSTRE	MUD	MOLE
pantone ® 13-1014	pantone ® 16-1328	pantone ® 16-1432	pantone ® 17-1040	pantone ® 18-1326	pantone ® 8561C	pantone ® 19-1420	pantone ® 18-1306

blue

ULTRAVIOLET	SEVRES	ELECTRIC	DUSK	MAUVE
pantone ® 19-3850	pantone ® 18-3935	pantone ® 18-4244	pantone ® 16-3919	pantone ® 18-3518

blue/grey

MIRAGE	DUCK EGG	SLATE	COQ	CHLORINE	INDIGO	PITCH
pantone ® 11-4802	pantone ® 12-4806	pantone ® 18-4510	pantone ® 19-5917	pantone ® 14-4814	pantone ® 19-4028	pantone ® 19-0303

yellow/green

ASTROTURF	CANARY	CATKIN	LEMONGRASS	PEA	SPEARMINT	ABSINTHE
pantone ® 16-6444	pantone ® 12-0752	pantone ® 15-0643	pantone ® 14-0223	pantone ® 17-0235	pantone ® 12-0317	pantone ® 16-5919

WGSN

COLOUR ANALYSIS

POROUS

JUMBLED

HALCYON

So___
A sof___

DEFINITIVE

eloquent   ashen   staged   brittle   granular

PITCH pantone ® 19-0303	BONE pantone ® 13-0513	TOMATO pantone ® 18-1445	WHITE pantone ® 11-0601	SLATE pantone ® 18-4510	ELEPHANT pantone ® 16-1107	CARAMAC pantone ® 16-1432	MOLE pantone ® 18-1306	INDIGO pantone ® 19-4028	COQ pantone ® 19-5917

JUMBLED

bri-collage   ceramic   conversational   jaunty   sentimental

SORBET pantone ® 17-1929	COPPER LUSTRE pantone 8561C	CORAL pantone ® 17-1547	BISCUIT pantone ® 13-1014	VANILLA pantone ® 12-0713	SEVRES pantone ® 18-3935	TEA pantone ® 16-1328	PEA antone ® 17-0235	DOVE pantone ® 15-4502	MUD pantone ® 19-1420

HALCYON

ssational   tinted   tender   evocative   poised

ROUND-NUT	ABSINTHE pantone ® 16-5919	CATKIN pantone ® 15-0643	FRESCO pantone ® 15-1512	MAUVE pantone ® 18-3518	PLUM pantone ® 18-1616	ALMOND pantone ® 13-0607	DUCK EGG antone ® 12-4806	DOVE pantone ® 15-4502	LEMON-GRASS pantone ® 14-0223

COLOUR PALETTES

POROUS

blanched   pigment   dry   scorched   pallid

ALABASTER pantone ® 11-0603	CACTUS pantone ® 16-0713	DESERT FLOWER pantone ® 16-1529	MIRAGE pantone ® 11-4802	BISCUIT pantone ® 13-1014	PLANTAIN pantone ® 12-0822	RED EARTH antone ® 16-1516	COFFEE pantone ® 18-1326	DUSK pantone ® 16-3919

58

INSPIRATIONAL MOOD BOARDS

8 Elliptical
Elliptical pull-on shape with slot-through neckline creates waterfall cascade folds to outside seams.

9 Teardrop
Teardrop silhouette with narrow shoulder-line and drop waist curving out to rounded full volume at hemline.

10 Square
Simplified form and symmetrical dimensions for oversized square-shaped knit.

SILHOUETTES

2 Coffe
A structu

the knee li

3 Bouf
An extre

1 Tailored afghan
A strictly tailored nappy short, squared-off dropped crotch, sharp pegged pleats and traditional tailoring details.

2 Coffee bean
A structured tailored pant with a curved outside leg seam that creates fullness around the knee line.

3 Bouffant
An extremely full-gathered skirt that creates bouffant-like volume.

1 Ruffles
Excess, meandering and contemporary

Excessive mass of ruffles

Wandering centipede

Contemporary

1 Amorphous cutting
Oscillating organic edges have a free-form fluidity.

5 Tubi-knit
Pull-on adaptable tubular knit coordinates create versatile body-conscious separates.

6 Jellyfish
A trapeze shape that combines diaphanous translucency with frilled organic layering volume for delicate fluttering volumes.

7 Kimono
Cropped boxy knit with wide bell sleeves creates a contemporary kimono-influenced silhouette.

SILHOUETTES

WGSN

RETAIL TALK

This Directory is aimed at buyers, merchandisers and designers, as well as visual merchandisers and marketers. Retail proves to be an increasingly directional and dynamic indicator of market, consumer and business future strength.

REPORTS offer commentary on store design and merchandising, covering leading global retail groups, chains and stores, as well as new retail concepts.

COMP SHOPPER offers information as is found in Trends.

CHAIN STORES/COLLECTION REVIEWS offers seasonal reports on trend-led and fast-fashion collections from the multiples and chain store sector.

BUYER INTERVIEWS offers strategies and brand/product choices from interviews with top-level buyers and design directors.

VISUAL MERCHANDISING offers information as is found in Trends.

Retail Talk has Scrapbook, Archive and Search functionality.

WHAT'S IN STORE

This Directory is aimed at all subscribers.

WGSN reporters travel the world shooting over 8000 photographs every month, covering all product areas, from men's, women's and childrenswear.

The cities covered monthly are London, New York and Paris. Additionally Milan, Tokyo and Los Angeles are covered every second month. Smaller seasonal reports are sent from such as Barcelona, Copenhagen, Antwerp, Amsterdam and Berlin.

SNAPSHOT reports are 'bite-sized' photo reports detailing the best a city has to offer.

RESORT REPORTS every summer, detail the glamour of St Tropez to the high summer beach and club scene of Ibiza.

Every thumbnail photo enlarges to allow hard copy printing for research or presentation purposes.

SLIDESHOW facility is available to allow the viewing of a whole product area.

HOT LOOKS reports provide a detailed view of the most directional retail trends. The latest colour, fabric, print stories and directional key items are highlighted. These are ideal for subscribers working close to a season.

VISUAL MERCHANDISING reports feature innovative window displays and the latest merchandising techniques. Seasonal promotions such as Christmas, Valentine's Day, Mother's Day and Easter are covered, highlighting gifts and decoration ideas.

Throughout the season new features are added such as, bridal, garden or denim.

COMP SHOPPER tracks key merchandise and promotions at shop floor level, with information on styling directions, prices, fabrics and promotions.

de leg seam that creates fullness around the knee line.

Harvey Nichols   Selfridges

bouffant-like volume.

STORE WINDOWS

Donna Karan
New York

Zuczug
Hong Kong

Cortefiel
Barcelona

Valentino
London

Helen Wang
New York

Wink
New York

Atsuro Tayama at IFC
Hong Kong

b+ab at Harbour City
Hong Kong

Diesel
New York

Nordstrom
London

On Pedder
Hong Kong

Jules Seltzer
Los Angeles

Butte
Indian-in

Soft
A soft, fl

DIRECTIONAL COLOUR

WGSN

CITY BY CITY

This Directory is aimed at the fashion and style business traveller.

Regularly updated Maps, Listings and Quick Guides of London, Paris, New York, Tokyo, Milan and Los Angeles offer the best places to visit. What's New lists the latest openings of bars, restaurants, clubs or galleries.

CITY GUIDES & TRAVEL offers inspiring destinations of the moment, key cities, resorts and 'hotspots' around the globe, including information on new stores, new places to eat and drink and the best hotels for a variety of budgets.

BITESIZE offers short updates on anything happening in travel, hotels and retail.

ART PULSE offers reviews of inspirational global exhibitions, art fairs and trends. 'Global Art Listings' updates listings for London, Paris, New York and other cities.

ROOM SERVICE offers an extensive hotel guide.

CATEGORY GUIDES offers groupings of product or sector specific reports in categories such as, interiors, vintage, childrenswear, youth/junior and activewear.

City By City has Scrapbook and Archive functionality with the addition of Report Search and Exhibition Search – a guide searchable by date, country and keyword; results appear with venue, date and exhibition contact details.

BEAUTY

This Directory is aimed at all subscribers as a key barometer of current and future trends.

REPORTS offers tracking of new looks from product laboratory to store counter and from catwalk to street. Beauty retail reports features developments in retail, technology, packaging and advertising.

HOT PRODUCTS offers focus on key launches, newest technologies, aromas, packaging ideas, advertising concepts and ingredients.

MARKET FOCUS offers the facts and figures that underline the developments in beauty.

KEY SEASONAL REPORTS offers key cosmetic brands' colour palettes through MAKE-UP COLOURS. Pantone shades reflect company products, photography and packaging. CATWALK VIEW tracks hair and beauty seen on the catwalks and MALE GROOMING features the latest information. TAX FREE WORLD and COSMOPROF exhibitions feature key trends, launches and products, WOMEN'S COSMETIC TRENDS links to seasonal cosmetic concepts developed by renowned make-up artist Sharon Dowsett.

BREAKING NEWS offers the latest updates on major events.

Beauty has Scrapbook, Archive and Search functionality.

LONDON   PARIS   NEW YORK   MILAN   TOKYO   LOS ANGELES   MORE CITIES

GLOBAL CITY REPORTS

Make-up

Giambattista Valli
Paris

Temperley
New York

Giorgio Armani
Milan

Dior

Nathan Jenden
London

John Galliano
Paris

Unconditional London

Bobbi Brown

MEN'S MILAN FASHION WEEK:
Street Report

Ashley Isham London

BEAUTY REPORTS

ACTIVE SPORTS

This Directory is aimed at designers, merchandisers, buyers and marketers. Sportswear has become one of the most vibrant and influential sectors of the fashion industry.

SEASONAL INFO offers a twice yearly overview of early colour palettes, key research and reference and seasonal inspiration. Directions in fabric/trims, graphics and key items and details are also provided.

TREND TRACKS offers emerging trends through photo reports from key sports events and locations.

REPORTS offers the latest information in technology, sports media and marketing, plus brand news and product updates.

RETAIL REPORTS offers key shopping cities reports and individual store reports.

TRADE SHOWS offers reports from ISPO, the Munich based event and other key international sports trade shows.

EDITOR'S CHOICE offers a monthly overview of inspiration.

BITESIZE offers short updates on the world of sportswear, news, inspirational brands, people, product, exhibitions and media.

Active Sports has Scrapbook, Archive and Search functionality.

YOUTH/JUNIOR

This Directory is aimed at designers and marketers.

This sector of the industry changes very quickly. Here WGSN try to identify underground trends that may have an impact on the broader market, influences include fashion, music, global cultural hot spots, up and coming artists, illustrators and street artists.

STREET offers hundreds of photographs gathered from around the globe. Reviews of key styling, colour, fabrics, print, pattern and knit are provided.

REPORTS offers new strategies, hot topics and campaigns from major brands to independent newcomers.

HOT STUFF offers information on 'hot' people, trends, ideas and designs along with attitudes, influences and destinations.

CITY ZONES offers the first indications of future trends from the world's style capitals from fashion to music, sport and entertainment.

BITESIZE offers short updates on inspirational people, brands, products, new media, magazines and hot trends.

EDITOR'S COMMENT offers specialist commentary on the month's important stories.

Youth/Junior has Scrapbook, Archive and Search functionality.

As seen at www.flickr.com   As seen at www.bryanappleyard.com

Rosa Chá, *Sport & Street Collezioni* spring/summer 2008

3 Bouffant

An extremely full-gathered skirt that creates bouffant-lik

ACTIVE SPORTS REPORTS

Girls' styling

Guys' styling

Metallic and sheen

Folk Fair Isle

Plaid and check

Graphic prints

Guys' jackets

Denim: surface and colour

Denim: grey and black

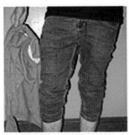

Denim: cropped

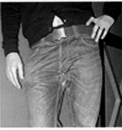

Denim: vintage look

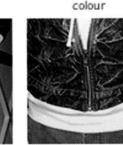

Denim: jackets

Denim: loose fit

Hats and scarves

Jewellery and accessories

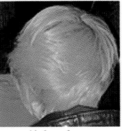

Hair colour

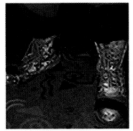

Footwear

Facial hair

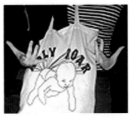

YOUTH/JUNIOR STREET REPORTS

WGSN

Denim is Everything Denim is Everything Edwin

Edwin Religion Religion

Revolution Boxfresh Ringspun

Roland Berry for Reebok Atticus Roland Berry for Reebok

Primary modernism

- White base with black and primary highlights
- Simplified, bold and linear
- Abstract cityscapes

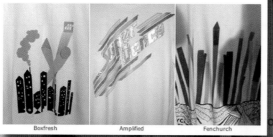

Boxfresh Amplified Fenchurch

GRAPHICS REPORTS

68

GRAPHICS

This Directory is aimed at graphic, print, and product designers, marketers and visual display specialists.

The information is 12 months plus ahead of the season and is designed to inspire the creative process.

Creative influences include fashion, art, music, film, global cultural hotspots, street culture and tastemakers.

COLLECTIONS offers an original library of sector specific conceptual collections in practical and usable artwork for logos and textile prints.

WGSN aim to make 80% of all collections available to download, as either Adobe Illustrator or Adobe Photoshop formats, with a view to the subscriber re-colouring or re-creating the original.

CLIPART offers a resource library to save time when searching for a specific image.

REPORTS offers the latest trends in typography, packaging, music, store and street and trade shows. Regular updates are also offered on directional agencies, graphic artists and illustrators.

BITESIZE offers short updates on everything happening in the world of graphics.

PACKAGING TRENDS offers seasonal packaging influences, shapes, inspiration, direction, materials and graphic themes.

TUTORIALS offers a series of design tutorials offering ideas for shortcuts and tips and tricks within computer aided design.

Graphics has Scrapbook and Archive functionality. Additionally Report Search is available and Image Search also. Downloadable Graphics are also offered in this Directory.

GENERATION NOW

This Directory is aimed at international design executives, marketers and advertisers.

This Directory is a showcase of graduating talent from some of the world's leading universities. It covers fashion, textiles, homewares, technology, product and auto design, photography, new media and film, including animation.

REPORTS offers features on exhibitions, work in progress, research and industry projects.

PORTFOLIO OF THE WEEK offers an opportunity for the best graduates to participate here. Each week a graduate is highlighted.

GRADUATE PORTFOLIOS offers online résumés and selected works by international graduates from the US, Europe and Asia, selected by their course leaders.

GRADUATE CATWALKS offers photo reports from the best graduate catwalk shows, highlighting innovative and fresh talent.

STUDENT BUZZ highlights the latest news and views, design university exhibitions and events.

Generation Now has Scrapbook, Archive, Calendar, Portfolio Search, Report/Catwalk Search functionality.

Soft cone

A soft, fluid A-line silhouette cre

GENERATION NOW – NEW TALENT

click on each image for larger images and slideshow

CARLIN INTERNATIONAL

Carlin International was founded in the 1940s by Fred Carlin whose creative flair and insight gave rise to a new type of agency built around style and fashion and a unique interdisciplinary approach.

In 1991 Carlin joined forces with 'Heure Locale' a leading communication agency. Today, Carlin Village is the strategic nerve centre, creative studio, fabric library, and mini house workshop located in the centre of Paris.

As both a design and advertising agency, Carlin International anticipates forthcoming trends, creates product lines and meets the communication needs of companies and brands. The concept of mixing trends with communication corresponds to the current expectations of professionals in the fashion business.

Carlin International combines its style, marketing and communication expertise to multiply its customer's sources of inspiration. Their 'know how' and synergy of talents enables them to develop comprehensive solutions tailored to individual projects. They provide personalised consulting services in addition to trends books.

The Carlin trend books are complete information guides that include major trends, colour, fabric and silhouettes twice yearly. The creative team of 30 international designers and researchers anticipate the trends of the future. They decode and predict emerging trend phenomena, develop brand strategies or product launches by forecasting macro and short-term trends, they interpret future seasons 2 years to 18 months ahead, and new consumer attitudes expected for 3-5 years ahead.

CHRISTINE LOYER, STYLIST OF CARLIN INTERNATIONAL

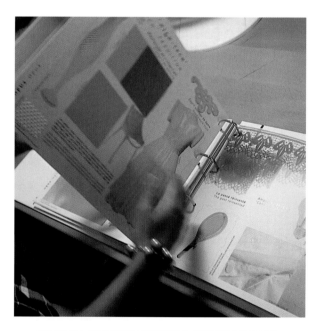

CARLIN INTERNATIONAL TREND BOOK

CARLIN INTERNATIONAL DESIGN
STUDIOS

RESEARCH & DESIGN AT CARLIN
INTERNATIONAL

The Carlin International team blends its interdisciplinary skills to build brand strategies, identify fashion trends, create product lines and communicate brand values. It engages a large range of expertise, employing staff as graphic artists, designers, stylists, colourists, photographers, multimedia developers, communication project managers, sales and marketing teams, creative writers, information specialists and press agents.

Their network of agents cover 25 countries ensuring the quality and range of their global watch. It provides a unique opportunity to test the validity of the trends identified and to take cultural differences into account.

STYLE AGENCY
The Style Agency develops customers' collections and brings creative solutions to projects through personalised consulting services.

COMMUNICATION AGENCY
This offers a comprehensive and imaginative approach to internal and external marketing communications, adding value to a brand's universe.

STRATEGIC CONSULTING
Strategic Consulting explores emerging markets and consumer attitudes, brand positioning strategy, consumer behaviour analysis, trend tracking validation by consumer groups and distributor surveys.

'EMULSIONCREATIVE'
'Emulsioncreative' is an independent subsidiary of Carlin International specialising in creative project management. It aims to rally a business team's creative skills and to ensure that their projects are explored constructively.

ABOVE – THE GRAPHICS STUDIO
CENTRE – FABRIC LIBRARY
RIGHT – COLOUR SWATCH LIBRARY

PAGES FROM SPORTS TREND BOOKS

AFFINITÉ
AFFINITY

TO FOLLOW THE MOVEMENTS OF THIS DANCER,
MOTIFS IMITATE ARABESQUES AND KNIT
USES RIB TRIMS.

ORIENTAL FEVER

SEXY TOPS

ADOPT A VERY ORIENTAL STYLE,
SILHOUETTE IS WRAPPED IN SCARVES
AND ADD A SPORT TOUCH, STRIPED
PUNCTATE THE OUTFIT.

CREATION CARLIN

TRÈS HAUTES / VERY HIGH

Maxi bord-côte rayé replié
Folded over, striped, maxi ribbing

Très haute et arrondie
Very high and rounded

Maxi et gainante
Maxi and body sculpting

TRÈS BASSES / VERY LOW

Basse, esprit smoking
Low, tuxedo style

Ultra basse et lacée
Ultra-low and lace-up

MINI

En biais
Slanting

Ronde et froncée
Round and gathered

Asymétrique
Asymmetrical

MAXI

Maxi poche kangourou
Maxi kangaroo pocket

Géante et zippée
Giant and zipped

Poche tranche

Dépliable et modulable

Porte-flûtes

Protège téléphone
Cell phone pocket

Porte carte géographique
Map holder

75

TRENDSTOP

Trendstop is an online forecasting company with a unique perspective and clientele. Here are two interviews: one with the CEO Jaana Jätyri, the other a day in the life of a Trendstop trend reporter.

INTERVIEW WITH TRENDSTOP.COM CEO JAANA JÄTYRI

1. What is Trendstop.com?
Trendstop.com is an online trend book. It is a web-based service that is updated with new trend looks, ideas and inspiration daily.

2. Where are you based?
Our trends are provided by a worldwide network of trend hunters. Our headquarters are in London, where we have a team of 20 trend researchers. Our global trend spotters are based in key cities around the world, e.g. New York, Los Angeles, Tokyo, Paris, Milan, Berlin, Barcelona.

3. What kind of information can you find at Trendstop.com?
For the online trend book, we focus on providing the latest trend information to our subscribers. We publish seasonal trend forecast stories and key trends analysed from runways, up-and-coming designers and street style. We also publish close-to-season forecasts for fast-fashion turnaround. Because we focus only on trend and have an experienced team, our forecasts are very accurate.

4. Who are Trendstop customers?
Our customers include celebrities, stylists, TV & movie production companies, designers and leading fashion brands and retailers worldwide.

+VERY ENGLISH & VERY ECO
+ELEGANT, E-AWARE & ENLIGHTENED
+BRILLIANTLY BOYISH WOMANLY WAISTLINES
+BRITISH TRADITION
+FRESH FUNKED UP FORTIES FEEL!!!

TWEED

This is definitely a look for the style savvy & its super kool to play with!!

Walter Van Beirendonck

STYLE INVASION

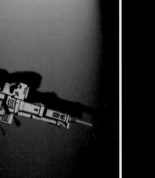

This is possibly the hottest story around right now so get ready to ride that gravy train and remember where you read it first!
Jean culture has been in the doldrums for quite a while now, with more products than customers. The problem? Well it all kinda looks the same and everyone already has them, so why buy what you already have!

L'Uomo Vogue 1988

BUBBLEGUM!

PH PHACTOR JUG BAND
the painted ship
seeds of time
NAL CIRCUS

Trendstop's "Tailor Of Gloucester"
This is pure inspiration and points t ev
to a reinvented concept of tailoring!
BEAUTIFUL! DESIRABLE! UNIQUE! U

TRENDSTOP

MATERIAL WORLD
EVERYTHING STARTS WITH AN...!

MATERIAL WORLD
LETS GET THIS PARTY STARTED u

TRENDSTOPS
KEY DECONSTRUCTION ELEMENTS!
CLOTHING WORN:
INSIDE OUT
UPSIDE DOWN
FRAYED
BURNT
SHREDDED
HANGING THREADS
SEAMS OUTSIDE
WITH HOLES

BEAUTIFUL!
ANDROGYNOUS!
POWERFUL!
POTENT!

PARAMILITARY URBAN GODDESS

77

This look celebrates the Belgian (Demeulemeester & Marg
& Japanese (Comme de Garçons, Yamamoto, Watanabe)
Designer Philosophies of androgyny to the full!

5. How do you forecast the trends? Are you creating the trends?

Trend forecasting is a form of market research. We track down the early adopters of new fashion looks, and based on our experience we'll draw conclusions on when a particular look is likely to hit the mainstream. This way we give our clients time to react to forthcoming trends, and get their collections ready in time for the demand.

6. Who decides about trends in colour, silhouette, fabric and pattern?

Trends are a common theme "in the air" at a given time, and the job of the trend forecaster is to be tuned in to the current "vibes" well enough to pick up what people are into and what they are going to be into. On more practical terms, we check out street style, clubs, fashion-forward stores, young designers, catwalks etc. to get intimate with what's going on in fashion.

7. How far in advance can you provide trend forecasts?

As opposed to providing just seasonal forecasts, we update our forecast stories weekly and monthly, providing a constantly evolving live document to our clients. In addition to mood-based seasonal forecasts, we are currently updating our forecast stories for Spring/Summer 2009. At the same time, we are also publishing close-to-season for Spring/Summer 2008 for those who need fast fashion ideas. We provide targeted product forecasts for specific product areas, such as Jeans, Accessories, Footwear, Lingerie, Tailoring, Street Sport, Shirts, Skirts, Dresses, Knits & Tees.

8. What about your global reporting?

We have a dedicated, hand-picked team of global reporters in key fashion capitals around the world, from New York to Tokyo and Helsinki to Sydney. They are constantly uploading pictures and reports to our trend HQ in London, where our trend team sort the information and publish it on the website.

9. Jaana, tell us about your background?

I come from Finland. I moved to London when I was 19 years old, because I wanted to study fashion. I graduated from Central Saint Martins (the famous fashion school, where Stella McCartney, Alexander McQueen and John Galliano studied) with first class honours in 1999.

During my internship I worked for a company that sells design software for the fashion industry. They trained me to use their software and sent me to train their London based customers on how to use the software. This was in the mid–90s and designers were very computer illiterate. As well as training, it became my job to help designers at high-street manufacturers to get their basic design shapes into the computer. I drew for them libraries of skirts, shirts, jackets etc. as well as all the detailing, such as pockets, collars, zips etc. to go with them.

I discovered that each company needed similar garment basics, so soon after I graduated I set up my first company, which would sell pre-made computerised design libraries for the fashion industry. My first clients were Marks & Spencer and River Island.

As well as basic shapes, designers wanted to know what the trend shapes were for next season – would skirts be pleated, frilly, short or long? So drawing trend shapes from the catwalks became a natural progression to the basic libraries.

Over the years the trend research team grew and eventually in 2004 it became our main business.

10. Who can use Trendstop?

Trendstop is used by all kinds of fashion and lifestyle companies, both large and small, as a product development and design tool. It's a bit like having your

BRIGHT PLAID
01.18 (TOKYO)

MAJORETTE
01.18 (LONDON)

PANDA ON PLAID
01.18 (LONDON)

PRINTED SNOOD
01.18 (TEL AVIV)

PRINTED SNOOD
01.18 (TEL AVIV)

FOOTBALL JUNK YARD RAVER
02.22 (TOKYO)

AIRBRUSH ANIMAL PRINT
02.09 (LONDON)

GOTHIC NAVY ROCKER
01.10 (NEW YORK)

SUITCASE MERCHANDISING
01.18 (LONDON)

ABOVE – STREET STYLE

own on-desk research assistant when you don't either have the budget to hire a full-blown research team, or the time to do all the global legwork yourself. Clients also use it to get presentation, visual merchandising, styling and photo shoot ideas.

11. How can you join Trendstop?

You can join online for a basic member-ship at www.trendstop.com. We have flexible options to choose customised packages that best suit each client's budget and requirements. We also provide additional content, customised updates and workshops for premium clients.

A DAY IN THE LIFE OF A TRENDSTOP TREND FORECASTER

1. Please can you tell me what your job entails?

I must confess that the life of a trend forecaster really is pretty much as you would expect: an endless procession of the most talked-about parties, fashion shows, new boutique openings, press days, talking to some seriously wild people in the street, continuous shopping, travelling around the world and discounts in our favourite stores to boot. On top of that a couple of hours at the laptop typing up what the spotter dragged in.

2. Who do you provide trend information for – ideally I'd like menswear labels.

Our clients include everyone who needs accurate, cutting-edge and commercially viable trend information, from freelance designers to global brands such as RipCurl and Billabong.

3. Are you given a brief by the brands as to what they are looking for, or do you just have to use your own judgement?

Both. We provide 'on spec' trend analysis for clients, as well as generic forecasts based on our global analysis of retail, street style, designer and social trends.

4. In an average working week, where do you go to look for trends, i.e. clubs, bars etc. How many hours do you spend doing this?

We are specialist trend spotters, so we really eat, breathe and sleep trends, 24/7 and whenever and wherever we are. This week we've been to London Fashion Week, Premiere Vision fabric show in Paris, Colette, the coolest store in Europe, pop concerts of Gwen Stefani and Prince, the 'Green is the New Black' launch in Hoxton, Doors and Concrete just off Carnaby St to spot the latest menswear trends and some vintage stores in Brighton.

5. What do you look for, what catches your eye?

When you are as focused on trend spotting as we are, it really becomes second nature, and you become naturally drawn to whatever is new and interesting. It really is like having invisible antennae that draw your attention to trend-worthy items like a magnet. When a good trend grabs you, you are powerless to resist the urge to follow...

6. Are you always mindful of the brand you are providing the information for?

We cover practically all the product areas: sportswear, jeans, tailoring, knitwear, accessories and footwear. Everyone in the team is focused on slightly different areas, and we all get together a huge pile of research, which we then dive into and dissect until we are able to spit out the answer to the latest trend looks, like an old main-frame computer. Because we have so much analysis and look at so many different angles, we don't really miss many tricks when it comes to spotting and describing trends. Of course when we are doing tailor-made projects for clients, then we take the clients requirements fully into consideration, and forecast specifically with their brand development, aspirations and target customer in mind all the way.

6. Do you take notes while there or do you write a report on your findings?

It depends on where you are. Sometimes if you can't carry it all in your head, it's good to take some notes down on your phone or by hand.

7. How difficult is your role considering there are so many potential trends out there?

We forecast trends as a full-time job, which extends to much of our waking hours, and that means that we spend probably ten times more time pondering and analysing trends than someone who just does it casually among their other activities. We are trained as mean, lean trend spotting machines, and nothing else interferes with that. That single-minded focus ensures that we are able to spot all the trends that matter, without breaking the proverbial sweat.

8. How did you get into the role?
I trained at Central Saint Martins, and if I hadn't gotten into trend spotting my goal would have been to become the next 'John Galliano'. I was a highly creative designer, but I didn't like pattern cutting, so trend forecasting allowed me to apply creativity on a purely intellectual level.

9. Do you find there is still a good fashion culture in the UK?
It's as good as, and mostly better, than anywhere. Those who search shall find.

10. Do you feel the UK is still leading the way?
It's becoming more of a global consensus with lots of different global spots having their contribution to the international mêlée of trend influences. But as a physical, rather than virtual location, London is still up there, and will be for some time to come.

11. Have you ever discounted looks that you knew wouldn't work?
You mean sorting the trash from the gold nuggets? We do that every minute of every hour, baby!

RIGHT – INSPIRATION TRENDSTOP STYLE

81

Представляем колонку
«What's Hot», которую
ведет Яна Ятури из
лондонского агентства
FashionRiot и ее
преданные трендхантеры

What's Hot

КАЖДЫЙ МЕСЯЦ мы будем информировать тебя
о самых горячих стрит-фэшн трендах, замеченных
на улицах Лондона и других больших городов. Так
что смотри what's hot, и непременно будешь в теме.

1 ОГЛЯНИСЬ НАЗАД

«По ту сторону ретро» – так можно
охарактеризовать модные очки этого
весенне-летнего сезона. Из каждой
декады берем по чуть-чуть – «кошачьи глазки» голливудских старлеток
50-х, 60-х: моды плюс Одри Хепберн и,
конечно, трэшовый нью-вейв 80-х.

2 ЗАЛЕЗЬ В ТРАНШЕЮ

Снова всплывают классические
тренч-коты. Для девочек – короткие
и приталенные, облегающие фигуру,
для мальчиков – средней длины или
небрежно скроенные короткие. Цвета:
черный, темно-синий, оливковый, или
классический бежевый, с закосом под
аутентичность.

3 LOUD&PROUD

Яркие, кроваво-красные или ядовито-
желтые аксессуары появляются во всех
модных клубах Лондона, Парижа
и Нью-Йорка. От туфель вишневого
цвета до неоновых дамских сумочек.
Массивный и заметный аксессуар – на-
стоящий must-have сезона.

TRENDSTOP

RUSSIAN STREET STYLE
TRENDSPOTTING FEATURE

4 ЭЛЕКТРИКА ВЫЗЫВАЛИ?

Шокирующий ярко-синий цвет «электрик» – настоящая встряска для всех предметов твоего гардероба. Одежда цвета «электрик» – претензия на серьезный стиль. Обтягивающий, пульсирующий и глубокий оттенок синего определенно добавит твоей внешности огня и поможет жечь.

5 ЧТО, ШКОЛЬНИЧКИ?

Облегающий блейзер на трех пуговках – обязательный элемент школьной формы в любой классической английской гимназии – для настоящих щеголей. Для достоверности не хватает только вышивки или эмблемы на нагрудном кармашке. А теперь – вперед покорять улицы больших городов.

6 СТАНЬ КОСМОНАВТОМ

Спортивная серебряная или золотая курточка – самая хитовая вещь для модного чела. «Космическое» происхождение цвета и покроя четко определит твой имидж космического бродяги. Самое важное – выбрать тусклые серебряный и золотой тона.

7 МАКСИ-ФАКТОР

Пряником из 70-х – возвращается мода на очень длинные юбки и платья. Молодые и уверенные в себе красотки ходят по улицам в длинных макси-юбках из элегантных струящихся материалов с золотыми принтами. Отдаленно напоминает яхты Сен-Тропе и коктейльную культуру 1973 года. Самое главное – крупные психоделические или ретро-принты.

8 ПЛОСКАЯ ПОДОШВА

Устав от нелепо и непомерно высоких каблуков и платформ прошлого сезона, этим летом девочки решили носить совсем плоские сандалии. Стиль – неоэтнический, с длинными вязанными или плетеными завязками, плетеным верхом и этническими принтами. Для тонко чувствующих моду.

9 УБЕЙ ЦВЕТОМ

Вместе с аксессуарами, очень яркие святящиеся цвета проникают в самые модные бутики, бары и клубы. Канареечно-желтый, вишнево-красный или изумрудно-зеленый – они могут быть основными, дополняющими или детальными. Яркие леопардовые принты и или крупные рисунки «со скатерти» – как раз то, что надо!

10 СЛОЕНАЯ ШЕЙКА

«Слоеный» стиль наконец-то дополз до украшений. Теперь модно носить бусы, колье и ожерелья разной длины, толщины, цвета и дизайна. Они придадут богенно-интригующий вид и отлично завершат твой безупречный стиль.

Эти и другие фэшн-тренды можно найти на наших сайтах fashionriot.com и trendstop.com. Наши трендхантеры работают в самых модных мировых городах и никогда не ошибаются.

Fashionriot.com – покажи миру свой стиль и создай свое собственное портфолио.
Trendstop.com – обязательный гид по модным трендам для профессиональных дизайнеров и просто одержимых модой.

OLD GOLD 15-0955 TPX

FLAMINGO 16-1450 TPX

MELLOW YELLOW 12-0720 TPX

FUSION CORAL 16-1543 TPX

CANTELOUPE 15-1239 TPX

PEACH BUD 14-1324 TPX

DAFFODIL 14-0850 TPX

CADMIUM YELLOW 15-1054 TPX

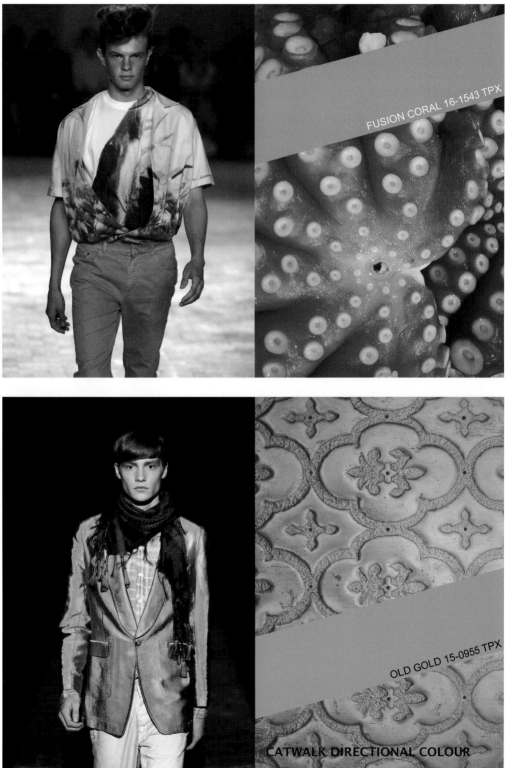

FUSION CORAL 16-1543 TPX

OLD GOLD 15-0955 TPX

CATWALK DIRECTIONAL COLOUR

PECLERS PARIS

Peclers Paris is a trend forecasting agency, offering a line of trend publications which preview and decipher consumer expectations for the fashion, interior and industrial design fields. Founded 30 years ago, Peclers Paris offers both consulting services and trend forecasting publications internationally. With an office in New York, as well as Paris, agents in Los Angeles, Miami and Canada, Peclers Paris adds extensive knowledge of the North American market to its expertise in the European and Asian markets.

From strategic planning to visual merchandising the team gets involved at each phase of the manufacturing process. Behind the scenes and in the field, they contribute to all levels of textile apparel, cosmetic, home and environmental design.

COMPANY PHILOSOPHY

Peclers Paris provide their clients with creative directions that add value to their offering and pragmatic solutions that correspond to their business needs. This ability to combine the analysis of 'transversal socio–cultural' currents with consumer and future insight and intuition brings tangible solutions to all markets.

CUSTOMISED SERVICE

Design, product development, visual merchandising, communication consulting.

BRAND STRATEGY

Analysis of a brand, its value and its marketing position plus recommendations.

CREATIVE COACHING

Creating key concepts with their clients, team colour, fabric and design direction.

RETAIL BUYING GUIDE

Ideas for product assortment and the editing of buying guides.

PRODUCT DEVELOPMENT CONSULTING

Concrete recommendations and development and support.

CONCEPTUALISATION OF COMMUNICATION TOOLS

Customised trend books, colour and fabric brochures.

VISUAL MERCHANDISING

Conceptualisation and realisation of window displays and trend forums.

Trend

Creative Intelligence

PeclersParis
A MEMBER OF THE **FITCH** GLOBAL STUDIO

PRODUCTS
The main business concerns working directly with the clients, supplying books and presentations and on consultancy projects. The website is an additional feature of Peclers' service. The designer collections are covered, but it is Peclers' editing and point of view that offers their unique perspective as to what is relevant and important information.

The publications cover:
Colour
Inspiration
Print and Patterns
Womenswear
Menswear
Childrenswear
Sportswear
Futures – Industrial design, media, telecommunications, motor industry.
Living – Homeware, retail sector, cosmetics, stationery, packaging.

87

LUCY HAILEY, BUSINESS PARTNER OF PECLERS PARIS – BASED IN LONDON

Lucy describes the philosophy and working practice of Peclers Paris and how the trend forecasting industry currently operates.

Working in the prediction industry is a complex job, it involves a unique combination of creative intuition, keen observation and market knowledge, every single person who works, contributing to Peclers' books, has had several years of experience as a project consultant working in specific market areas. The head office in Paris carries a 60 strong team managed by senior heads of both design and marketing. An international network of professionals service more than 26 countries and Peclers publish 20 key seasonal forecasting publications per year. Their main clientele are from the textile, apparel, cosmetic, home and environmental design industries.

WHAT MAKES PECLERS INDIVIDUAL?

Peclers is the 'Rolls Royce' of trend forecasting; they provide a customised service advising on all facets of design, product development and communication consulting.

LONDON OFFICE

From strategic planning to visual merchandising the team is involved at each stage of the manufacturing process helping each client to confirm their uniqueness and develop innovative strategies.

IMPORTANCE OF COLOUR

Peclers are renowned for their colour direction. Manufacturers, retailers, yarn and textile industries use colour as the starting point of the design and selection process. Experience and judgement is essential in selecting the right palette and colour stories, as colour can make or break a season. Colour is taken very seriously in industry, and can be agonised over – you think you have the 'right' red and then find out that you have the 'wrong' one after all! The decision can be disastrous for that season's sales figures; big brands and retailers can loose millions over the wrong colour palette.

Peclers produce a colour book 'Colours' that forecasts two years ahead, a seasonal colour palette, colour combinations and market specific colour cards.

DIRECTIONAL COLOUR WORK

New materials, patinas and finishes support the inspirational visuals. Their clients love the tactile feel of the books that contain fabric, colour and textural samples on each page.

The palettes described within the Colour Book are translated into the other publications as the season progresses and is updated.

INSPIRATION

The 'Inspirations' book is an essential tool for the luxury industries; it gives a preview of the season's concepts from a fashion point of view. This is initiated by the heads of each division creating a 'think tank' meeting where each brings their creative intuition and experience of important art events. Architecture, exhibitions, cultural hotspots, colour or technological developments are discussed to form the basis of the Inspirations book. This book is the most wide ranging and is sold to all sectors of the design industry.

EDITING

Forecasting publications are essential in the forward planning process for industry. They assist design and selection by editing the huge amount of information in the marketplace, in an experienced and precise manner. Many large companies and brands buy information from a number of forecasting agencies in order to verify and confirm their own predictions on which direction fashion trends, within their own specialist market sector, will evolve. Some companies employ specialist staff to edit information in-house.

There are now very fast lead times in manufacturing production allowing fashion brands to develop looks quickly from analysing their own market or copying designer collections and samples from around the world. There is an overload of information available and it is difficult for designers to sift through in order to make an informed decision. Consumers are increasingly sophisticated and confident now so precise decisions are crucial. It is the role of Peclers to cut through the things that are irrelevant, to edit information from the overload sifting. It is also the job of the forecaster to predict downturn in popular trends too, to pinpoint the moment when the trend starts to descend the hill.

THE ROLE OF THE AGENT

Peclers carefully select their agents – called Business Partners, they all have extensive marketing knowledge and come from creative backgrounds. Their role includes supplying publications, presentations and providing additional support and guidance to customers. They have six-monthly meetings at Peclers where the team are introduced to the seasons publications and are talked through the key influences for the coming season. This is important as they may have three seasons 'on the go' at one time – Spring just finishing, Winter current and the following Spring.

Companies work in a variety of ways, for example, updating from the previous season; some retailers don't wait, they will use information ahead of the season if they have confidence in the story. Head Office, in Paris, listen to the agents out in the field analysing feedback, listening to the positives and negatives about what customers are feeling about the products.

HOW DOES INDUSTRY UTILISE THE INFORMATION?

FASHION INDUSTRY

Leading fashion manufacturers and retailers subscribe to a number of prediction companies' books and on-line reportage; although these are expensive they offer confirmation of decisions taken about the forthcoming designs and it is important to be as well informed as possible in order to stay ahead of the competition.

Silhouettes

FULL FIGURE 'LOOKS'

When new trends arrive they are often in a raw state and can be quite challenging for the client to appreciate as they may be at odds with the current zeitgeist, as time moves on they are developed into something really special and become much more palatable. Confirmation of an instinctive feeling for a trend helps to sell it. They start predicting two years ahead of the season and the new can be quite shocking, for example, simple colour blocking when 'Boho' was in fashion.

The books are there for designers, they are full of really good knowledge that will make the extra millions for your companies, they use forward information to reach out and put themselves ahead of the competition.

Designers have to learn how to interpret the information for their market area, skillfully decoding, translating and rendering the results and having a 'feeling' for colour etc., that is in essence 'creativity'. Designers who know how to use the books fall in love with images. Long-term trends are easier to track than some of the more fickle youth market trends that may be music related.

BROADER DESIGN INDUSTRY

The wider design and service industries utilise fashion forecasting information, this includes web and graphics, media transport, telecommunications. These companies need trend information to understand the industries that they are supplying. Design has become a much more central focus now, within company structure, than it was ten years ago, it is recognised that if you don't invest the time, if you don't have a design department or buy in information, your company may be at a serious dis-advantage. Design can change the face of products for the better, making them beautifully considered, that are fit for purpose, or more ecologically sound, enriching the consumer's experience.

GLOBAL MARKETS

Peclers constantly assess emerging client bases, for example, China, Poland and South America. These newly expanding markets are providing opportunities for a variety of design services. These are required by developing countries not only to support manufacturing, but to understand the design and service industries.

92

PECLERS PARIS OFFICE

CONCEPTS PARIS
LINGERIE CONSULTANTS

Concepts Paris is a leading lingerie design source.

As an influential trend forecasting and design consultancy, they design and report on all aspects of body-fashion; serving global leaders in manufacturing and retailing, they offer trend books and design and marketing concepts based on their own studies of how the lingerie market is developing.

Concepts philosophy has developed an understanding of today's woman, as an intelligent informed and cultured consumer. The company believe that suppliers of consumer goods today are actually part of the entertainment industry; collections are themes and stories to tell, so it is important that they are innovative, exciting and create a 'buzz' for the prospective consumer.

TREND BOOKS
The trend books combine creative challenge with inside information, 18 months ahead of retail, for key people: trend directors, designers, merchandisers, marketing directors, brand managers.

BOOK: SIGNS OF CHANGE
This book analyses current commercial trends, creating advanced colour, fabric & print ideas plus the main design themes for the new season, for range building & collection strategies. A shop report examining market trends is created from information researched at trade fairs; information is expertly edited including photographs of collections. This expresses Concepts' viewpoint alongside inspiration for clients. This is issued in March and September.

BOOK: DESIGN CONCEPTS
This is Concepts' main trend book, creating an insight into the most important new trends presented in inspirational silhouettes.

The four trends are developed from 'Signs of Change' and are developed into specific design ideas with inspirational imagery and fabric samples covering designer and volume markets. These include exclusive photographs of catwalk designer influences, merchandising and packaging ideas, advanced colour stories, fabric swatches and print developments. This is issued in May and November.

CONSULTANCY
Fabric and garment manufacturers, brands and retailers commission special projects from Concepts Paris who supply a full design service.

This ranges from specific trend information, help & advice on design, sourcing and merchandising issues, tailored to clients market level and location, to website updates, specialist shopping guides, and reportage on trade fairs in Paris, Lyon, Shanghai and Hong Kong.

BACKGROUND FROM THE INTERFILIÈRE & LYON, MODE CITY PUBLICATION

UPDATE

Evolution

NOW
UPDATE
PREVIEW 07/08

INTERFILIÈRE & Lyon, Mode City 2006

23 CAMPANULE BLUBELL 24 MARINE MARINE 25 ORAGE THUNDERSTORM

THE EVOLUTION TRENDS BOOK

Concepts help to create this trend publication, designed for the trade fairs Interfilière, Paris, and the Salon International de la Lingerie. This book offers all the key details of a continually evolving market.

COLOUR

Colour is one of the most important elements of lingerie design and also its interaction with materials. These influences are often taken from streetwear and interiors as a source of inspiration.

The colour card is the name given to pre-selected colour stories chosen for the forums of trade fairs.
The colours are chosen by a group of lingerie specialists, twice a year; experts arrive with mood boards and discuss their opinions about colour along with consumer trend and current attitudes towards colour sales; these are put into themes and form displays which are intended to focus and inform visitors, from industry, of forthcoming trends.

Couleurs Interfilière 07/08

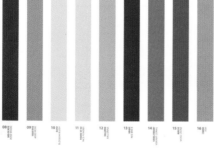

FABRICS

As there is less opportunity to change cut with lingerie, the design of the fabrication itself is paramount. This involves in-depth experimentation and partnerships with textile manufacturers. Each season specialist lingerie fabric manufacturers develop and expand their ranges through pattern, colour and texture, handle and perfomance.

New designs can be entirely driven by innovative developments in technology; organic, mouldable, embossed, thermoregulating, stain-resistant, heat-bonded or slimming fabrics, laser-cutting, spacer fabrics and 'cuttable' lace, for example. Manufacturers need to remain informed of changes in consumer behaviour and invest astutely in appropriate technology to maintain market position.

LINGERIE TRADE FAIRS

The trade shows are designed to open up new horizons for lingerie designers, retailers and manufacturers facilitating access to new markets and exchanging experience with other lingerie professionals.

SALON INTERNATIONAL DE LA LINGERIE

Salon International de la Lingerie is the the largest trade fair for lingerie and is held in Paris. Lingerie buyers, designers, textile manufacturers and lingerie brands from all over the world visit the fair to sell and research. This is where brands and designers will sell their collections to buyers for the next Autumn/Winter season.

INTERFILIÈRE

Interfilière is held in Paris and Lyon. This fabric and trimmings fair presents the very best on offer, from the world of lace, embroidery, knitted fabric, woven fabric, ribbons, trimmings and accessories bringing the most innovative fabrics together for optimal effect. It attracts approximately 25,000 professionals, exhibitors and visitors.

Au Musée
Museum pieces

A l'œuvre : le passé le plus précieux et authentique,
XVIIIè siècle en tête. Autant de tableaux et toiles de
maître où puiser le nouveau raffinement.

Mini boutons empruntés à la
noblesse XVIIIè.
Mini buttons borrowed from the 18th

Dentelle d'aujourd'hui mais alliée
aux imprimés boudoirs.
Modern lace mixed with boudoir

La taille Empire comme nouvelle ligne
à suivre.
Keep an eye on developments of the.

Robinson
Moderne
Modern Robinson

Flous artistiques, tonalités délavées de kaki et de jean, effets fait main et customisés, effilochés ou déchirés.

Diluted tones of khaki and denim, hand-made and customised, torn effects.

Bacus

UPDATE

A wardrobe of cover-ups for beach fashionistas

Garde-robe complète pour fashionistas

EVOLUTION
INTERFILIÈRE & LYON
Concepts create four stories, each with six themes for their 'Update' section.

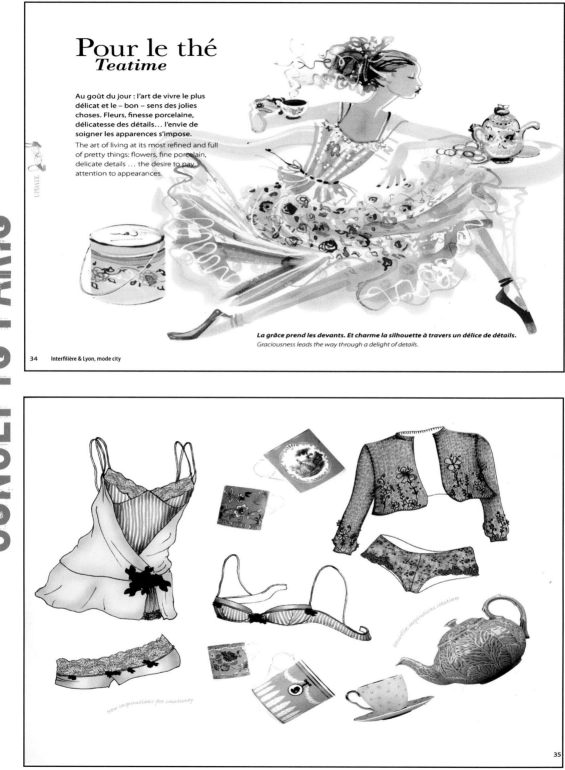

Pour le thé
Teatime

Au goût du jour : l'art de vivre le plus délicat et le – bon – sens des jolies choses. Fleurs, finesse porcelaine, délicatesse des détails… l'envie de soigner les apparences s'impose.

The art of living at its most refined and full of pretty things: flowers, fine porcelain, delicate details … the desire to pay attention to appearances.

La grâce prend les devants. Et charme la silhouette à travers un délice de détails.
Graciousness leads the way through a delight of details.

34   Interfilière & Lyon, mode city

35

Fleurs ornementales
Decorative flowers

L'esprit papiers peints continue de plus belle et de plus fleuri.
Motifs arabesques, rondes de pétales, effets pochoirs, alliances
botaniques impriment partout leur radieuse élégance.

Wallpaper looks continue with the flowers more beautiful than
ever. Arabesques, petals, stencil effects, botanical mixes cast their
elegant radiance everywhere.

Weisbrod-Zuerrer

117

Anthropologie

Hanna Werning

Interfilière & Lyon, mode city

Anthropologie

LI EDELKOORT & TREND UNION

Lidewij (Li) Edelkoort is a leader in the 'science' of trend forecasting. She is Directrice of Studio Edelkoort and founder of Trend Union, the style bible for anyone involved in design.

Li is Dutch by birth, but Parisienne by adoption. She describes herself as lucid in trend forecasting.
For almost 15 years she has created and directed a bureau that provides trend information to companies in every sector, for textiles to automobiles to cosmetics.

Li announces the colours and materials that will be in fashion two or more years from now:
"Because there is no creation without advance knowledge and without design a product cannot exist". In this way she orientates professionals in interpreting the evolution of society and the foreshadowing signals of consumer tastes to come, without forgetting economic reality.

Li travels constantly, listening, shopping and searching the world over, she taps into everything. Political, ethnological, artistic, literary and consumer movements all come under her scrutiny for analysis.
She is internationally known and respected, her authority and influence encompass conceptual forecasts of trends in Fashion, Interiors and Product design.

She sits on the steering committees for the larger European Textile shows and participates in the selection of colour and trends. She has also been a visiting Professor at the Royal College of Art in the United Kingdom. She is a member of the editorial board of Elle Decoration and voted by The Face magazine as one of the top 50 influences in the world of style. She is Director of the Eindhoven Design Academy in the Netherlands.

The Edelkoort philosophy is based on consensus and as she explains "the days when one held the hand of industry are finished. I want to do what I do with as much integrity as possible and not always be saying what people want to hear. I also want to stimulate the creativity in people...and not to dictate rules, only to give a general framework".

TREND UNION

Trend Union was formed to create trend books in 1986, under Li's directorship. This is an association of 10 designers and stylists. Each has their own professional activities within different sectors of the Fashion and Interiors industry.
At the beginning of each season, these professionals meet, bringing personal reflections, views and materials to define the trends and the colours of the future.

TREND BOOKS

The Trend Books are arranged into themes, illustrated with diverse materials, such as photographs, fabric, swatches, yarns, threads, newspaper clippings, objects and gadgets to suggest trends. Often they are accompanied by specialist booklets which focus on a particular trend in detail. The trend books are purchased by a diverse range of clients in the fields of Architecture, Automotive, Cosmetics, Fashion, Accessories, Interiors and Textiles in manufacturing, design, marketing and retail.

In today's competitive world, these books act as a vital aid to companies striving to keep ahead in their particular markets. They inspire and inform, enabling clients to formulate their own design and marketing strategies. The titles include: Colours & Colour Tool, General Trend Book, Men's Colours, Pattern Book, Touch-fabric, the Beauty Book, the Key, Well Being Bible and the Lifestyle Book.

LI EDELKOORT

PRESENTATIONS & SEMINARS

Every season an audio-visual presentation is held in the Studio, in Paris, at about the time of Premiere Vision fabric fair. In addition, audio-visual trend presentations take place in Japan, Scandinavia, USA and the UK.

WORLDWIDE

Trend Union have representative agents in Australia, Austria, Belgium, France, Spain, Germany, Holland, Italy, Japan, Korea, Netherlands, Taiwan, United Kingdom and the USA.

MAGAZINES

Li also established a publishing company to create VIEW ON COLOUR and INVIEW magazines for design professionals. Subsequently she launched BLOOM, a trend magazine, aimed at the flower and plant industry, but with a much wider appeal.

OTHER SERVICES

• Private showings of the Trend Union Audio-visual Presentation.
• Consultation with one of the Trend Union members.
• Conception and realisation of specific project dossiers.
• Realisation and Presentation of Trend Forums.
• Conferences with Li Edelkoort.

Recent clients have included Nissan, Mooi, Camper, Gucci, Philips, Coca Cola, Estée Lauder, Swatch, Lancôme and Wella.

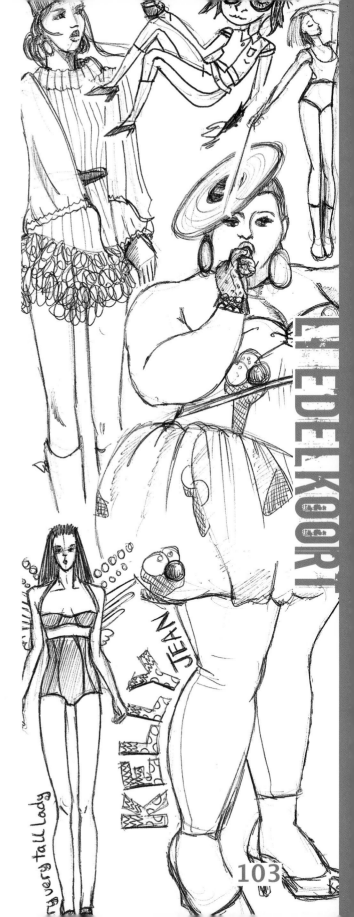

LI EDELKOORT

103

FASHION FORECASTING COMPANIES: PROMOSTYL
www.promostyl.com

Promostyl is a global trend forecasting agency with headquarters in Paris and a network of agents worldwide. Centering on lifestyle trends, Promostyl gives adaptations for all markets with colour and silhouette direction with a balance of creativity and commercial viability. Around for almost 40 years, Promostyl works with major companies in all fields: Apparel, Beauty, Automotive, Consumer Products and more.

Promostyl brings to its customers solutions 18 to 24 months in advance. The Colors, Influences, and Fabrics trend books present the four main themes that will define each season. These four chief themes are then detailed, enriched and adapted for the specific market of each book.

Richly illustrated with drawings, sketches and photos, these books offer realistic and precise views of the future of clothing trends. Published in English, French, Japanese, and for some in Chinese, they come with textile swatches and product presentations on CD-Rom. An invaluable source of inspiration, logos and exclusive prints are also included in their books in a user friendly format.

INFOMAT – THE FASHION INDUSTRY SEARCH ENGINE
www.infomat.com

InfoMat collaborates with the best international colour and trend service providers in the fashion industry. Together with top fashion forecasting companies, they present a trend fashion forum that keeps retailers and manufacturers current. Find trend analysis, street style, store windows, runway and trade show reports along with consumer trends that forecast the future of fashion design and retail sales. They track over 3500+ events in the global fashion industry each year.

MILOU KET STYLING & DESIGN
www.milouket.com

Milou Ket Styling & Design is based in Purmerend in the Netherlands. Milou Ket provides a range of trend books called, Interiors, Innovation Lab, Interior Colours and Womens Trends. She has extensive experience in the field of consultancy. After an initial introduction, she formulates the client's needs. This is dependent upon market position, image, target groups, price level, competition, location and company strategy.

Milou visits several international capitals for shopping, she reads consumer and trade magazines and visits trade fairs. She is a member of different fashion institutes and visits international trend lectures.

A tailor-made styling report is presented, based on current and future trends concerning style direction, colours, materials, prints and finishes, shapes and other important items. Upon request a collection plan can be made and realised together with buyers or merchandisers. Milou Ket can also design prints and indicate colourways and colour combinations.

NELLY RODI
www.nellyrodi.com

Nelly Rodi is a colour trend agency that specialises in publishing catalogues designed to assist creative teams and manufacturers as they develop future product lines.

With expertise in the textile, packaging, automotive and cosmetic industries, this Paris based company has been helping design teams through their creative processes since 1985. With a team of 28 forecasting professionals travelling the world in search of new colours and design ideas, the agency has become renowned for its exceptional ability to provide designers with a rare insight into future consumer trends.

FASHION SNOOPS
www.fashionsnoops.com
Fashion Snoops was created by a group of designers with a vision to bring market and trend intelligence to fashion and style related companies.
Established in 2001, Fashion Snoops offers its customers a unique combination of up-to-the-minute trend knowledge and global research power that can be assigned to specific projects.

Online fashion trend services Fashion Snoops is the creator of fashionsnoops. com, the US-based online forecasting and trend analysis service. The service provides fashion companies with practical and timely answers to the burning question of 'what direction should my line take next season?' It supports fashion professionals with fresh information from the international runway, trade show and retail scenes, as well as with in-depth analysis on up-coming trends in design themes, colours, key bodies, graphics, and more.

COLOR PORTFOLIO INC
www.colorportfolio.com
Color Portfolio is an American colour and trend company. It has been in existence for 20 years; Color Portfolio offers colour and trend books to retailers, manufacturers and allied industries, providing directional and understandable recommendations for successful colour, trend, and textile merchandising.
In addition to producing four seasonal market colour books, 'Essence of Color' (formally called Color Portfolio), 'Thinking In Color', 'On The Edge', and 'Color Portfolio Kids', various seasonal trend reports are created. Color Portfolio also offers personalised design and trend reports for companies with specific market needs. Color Portfolio's client base consists of noteworthy retailers, apparel manufacturers, and textile companies in all market areas, including both domestic and international markets.

OTHER KEY PLAYERS

105

STYLESIGHT
www.stylesight.com

Stylesight is a New York based company that covers, fashion design, trend analysis, forecasting, reporting, merchandising and apparel manufacturing.

Their mission is to provide clients with the tools to improve their creative and product development process, tools that help efficiency, economics, accuracy and promptness to market.
They achieve this by offering a global reaching, time sensitive, informative and directional website.
Their content provides everything a merchandiser and designer need to assess current trends, collaborate and analyse their trend forecasts and report for effective results during the design cycle.

STYLELENS

www.stylelens.com

This is an American subscription based online service providing global fashion news, trends and forecast reports for clothing and apparel manufacturers, retailers, schools and freelancers and any other interested parties that require quick access to information.
Stylelens covers Japan, Los Angeles and all the major European fashion capitals, using sketches, photos and movies.

FASHION FORECAST SERVICES
www.fashionforecastservices.com

This Australian based business has been operating since 1991 and offers international reports for colour and trend services to the fashion, homewares and associated industries.
Their client base extends throughout Australia and New Zealand. They offer reports on women's, men's, childrenswear, accessories, textiles, homewares and interior markets. These reports are supplied to major retailers, manufacturers, wholesalers and importers.

JENKINS REPORTS UK
www.jenkinsuk.com

Jenkins is a London based, established colour and trend forecasting company with an international client base including major retailers and key brands in fashion, home, gifts, beauty and leisure products. Their main aim is to always provide a strong working tool, inspirational, easy to use and commercial.

Their team of forecasters have been observing and interpreting the factors driving consumers moods and desires for over 15 years.
Each season they start with their early thoughts on colour and mood which they expand into a fully developed range of colour and design trend forecasts for fashion and interiors, released seasonally and swatched with Pantone TCX and yarns.

Jenkins' well established (since 1992) CLICK Fashion & Lifestyle retail reports are now web-based, combining the latest images from trade shows, stores and street with an edited, targeted view of the most directional design.
They have a journalistic viewpoint on key stories, items and trends in mainstream fashion and interiors. They have a search tool on the website which enables the user to browse over 2500 images or input keywords.
All of the images and stories may be downloaded as PDFs (portable document format).

Click Fashion has an edited overview of international retail trends, focused on mainstream fashion and targeting key items, shapes, details, fabrics, prints and colour for the average woman.

Click Lifestyle has an overview of international home product trends at retail and at trade shows, examining new directions for gifts and interior design, with the focus on colour, print/pattern and texture.

Christmas decorations are also included.

They also provide updated shop lists for fashion and interiors covering major international cities.
Their biannual seasonal presentations examine the main cultural and emotional influences behind key design trends.
They also provide customised projects including targeted research and presentations.

TREND BIBLE
www.trendbible.co.uk
Trend Bible is based in Newcastle upon Tyne and is considered the first comprehensive book for the interiors, gift and packaging industry.
They use a 'magpie' approach to trend forecasting where they combine the work of up and coming designers with exclusive vintage finds. This blend offers inspiration to designers and buyers alike, highlighting the defining products within each trend.

They also provide advanced market and consumer research, highlighting the most significant information for a client's needs. They provide up-to-the-minute forecasts for the client to make informed decisions, minimising risks. They understand the ever evolving customer.

They publish two books a year, each featuring the four key trends of the season and subscribers have access to their online trend service.
Their books come complete with original imagery, Pantone® referenced colours and swatches of wallpaper, fabric, flooring and gift materials.
Their books have a distinctive, sketchbook-like quality, reflected also in their website design.

Whilst not a fashion led company, the following company works with brands and consumer lifestyle information like many trend oriented companies. The tools are different but the message has to be contemporary and appeal to the consumer.

BRANDNEWWORLD
Creative Solutions Company
www.brandnewworldus.com

Brandnewworld are an eclectic mix of artists, musicians, film fanatics, sports-nuts and heady intellectuals. They are from far reaching places like Russia, Peru and even Cleveland.

Their expertise includes Interactive Advertising Campaigns, Brand sites filled with original video content, Identity Design and Experience Packaging across print, digital, and on-air animation, applications, cutdowns, events, man-on-the-street, mobisodes, presentations, sales strategy, viral and other creative experiences for emerging technologies and mediums.
They focus on messages that cross 'platforms' and cultures.
They don't differentiate between campaign ideas that are conceived for the web versus those that are created for traditional channels. Regardless of the platform, they approach all projects with the same level of expertise and ingenuity.

THEIR PHILOSOPHY:

ON THE MARKETPLACE
Rapid innovations in technology yield rapid development of new media channels, while further fragmenting the already divided attentions of the consumer. Elevating the messaging above the noise requires creative solutions that are not only visible, but are profoundly felt over time. Consumer participation in the brand narrative is necessary for sustaining cultural

relevance and it is important to begin with weighty emotional brand ideas that are compelling and evocative, regardless of the delivery technology.

ON DIGITAL IN THE MEDIA MIX
Brandnewworld begin by ensuring that their strategic and creative ideas are anchored by a compelling Brand Story, which, in turn, is differentiated through a higher order benefit to the consumer, and grounded in authentic cultural experiences.

Then they ensure the messaging is where the consumers are whether on or off a website. It is a matter of creating a wealth of creative elements that enable the Brand Story to travel far and wide.

ON PARTNERSHIP
They listen.
It is the launching point from which they gain understanding of the brand and the objectives. They then refine their insights and brainstorm on the optimal approach to meet needs, ensuring that their proposed solutions are grounded in strategic direction, vision and insights, and achieve communication objectives by being clear, concise and focused. They then experiment by prototyping a wide range of creative concepts, and refine till they have the best solutions for messaging needs. Finally, they execute – with a strong dedication to production value and measurable results. Then they listen some more.

There are companies set up, all over the world, to represent other trend and fashion forecasting companies; such companies are called 'Agents' or 'Business Partners' in the case of Lucy Hailey and Peclers.

Agents may also set up trend presentations for clients and send out email updates, in the form of newsletters, regarding products and services.

KM ASSOCIATES
http://kmauk.com/index2.html

KM Associates are a colour, lifestyle and trend information bureau. For over 16 years they have been the UK marketing, PR and sales agents for the most highly regarded sources in France:

Li Edelkoort: Colour and Trend consultant
Trend Union: Trend books
Studio Edelkoort: Design Studio
Gert Van de Keuken: Creative Director, Studio Edelkoort
Edelkoort etc.: Other Edelkoort activities, seminars and workshops
View on Colour: Colour and trend magazine
Bloom: Horticultural/plant trend magazine
Edelkoort Editions: Publisher and image library

They are also UK agents for other colour, trends and design studios/services including:

Milou Ket: Dutch interiors trend/design studio
Jenkins UK: UK fashion and interiors trend studio

They deliver information to their clients through channels such as:

Trend Books
Trend Magazines
Trend Presentations
Consultancy.

fastest driver on Earth

officially

ANDY GREEN

OTHER KEY PLAYERS

109

THE INSPIRATIONAL MAGAZINE

Subscribing to fashion forecasting materials requires an investment by a company. It is recognised by most fashion companies nowadays that this is an essential tool rather than a luxury, and is no longer fortune to the 'ups' and 'downs' of the fashion industry. However, there are other methods of gaining inspiration that may be considered more accessible, more frequent and more affordable, but are not a substitute for more exclusive publications and consultancy. This inspiration is through the magazine market. Not magazines that are available on the newsagents shelves, although larger stores do sell them, but available through subscription, at trade fairs and through specialist suppliers. These are substantial magazines that explore colour, texture, fabrication, recent catwalk reports and retail; this could be from the point of view of window displays, shop architecture and interiors, the selling experience and last but not least, the actual merchandise/ product sold within.

Because of their affordability fashion students tend to invest in this type of material. There is often high concept content as well as straightforward reportage, but the editorial of each magazine will have a particular angle. For example, the inspirational magazines, like Provider and Wear, will show the more extreme directional elements of catwalk collections and retail, whereas the View series will arrange collections into more general stories and themes that help to re-inforce directions previously forecast.

WeAr – CONTENTS AND CATEGORIES – 2008

MODE INFORMATION
mode...information
Heinz Kramer GmbH
www.modeinfo.com
Agents for Forecasting Products

Mode Information are a specialist supplier who provide a range of books, magazines and online services especially for textile, fashion, graphics, interior, architecture and lifestyle industries. They also provide all of the Pantone® products for exact colour communication. They offer consulting services with focus on colour and surface design, trend seminars and workshops for all product areas.

HISTORY
The company was founded in Overath near Cologne and was based on the idea of finding early trend information.
The company's founder Heinz Kramer, discovered, around 50 years ago, that there was too much fashion information available, so he decided to select and edit the information and make it available to others to save them time. The company supplied information on trends and associated materials to the design industry so securing crucial competitive advantages for its clients. Today Mode Information is managed by Yann Menard and Dr Jens Schumacher, the business is continuously expanding and is today regarded as one of the top trend materials suppliers worldwide.

PHILOSOPHY
They acquire the items of information from the design, product development, product management or marketing fields. They owe their success to their excellent service and their systematic product selection and they work closely with the fashion industry's creative trend-setters.

Spanning the entire world, their sales network covers the global market for trend-relevant data.

SOME EXAMPLES OF PUBLICATIONS AVAILABLE FROM MODE INFORMATION

FROM LEFT – TEXTILE VIEW, WEAR

mode...information – ideas ahead of time

mode...information – the professionals' first choice

111

WEAR GLOBAL MAGAZINE
www.wear-magazine.com

WeAr describe themselves as a conceptual and professional magazine. The publisher and editor is Klaus Vogel:

> "Couture meets leisurewear, symbiosis of art and fashion, visual information instead of long-winded texts, facts instead of personal opinions.
> The reader is presented with the most interesting collections, stores and market news world wide. Editorial content, fashion, shoes and accessories for the high-end segment.
> Editorial mainstay: shops and trend reports from the world's major cities and from trade fairs, supplemented with news, research, contacts, interviews, business talk, tips, focused on the very best."

The emphasis is on the visual coverage of:
Relevant stores, showrooms, display windows, interior furnishings, product presentations.
Look book: photographs of shows and the latest from the most important trade fairs in the world.
Trend Reports from the major cities, people, stores, lifestyle.
Photographs of designer collections and trends.

> "Art and the zeitgeist inform the issue's presentation, its cover, information is accordingly clear, accessible, vivid, professional. The texts on the various topics, as well as the interviews, are short and to the point. They benefit the reader by providing them with information which increases their turnover, improves business or confirms what they already know."

The publication is truly global and is translated into eight languages, English, German, Spanish, Italian, French, Mandarin, Japanese, Russian.

TOP – MAGAZINE SPREAD
DIRECTLY ABOVE – CONTENT OF THE OPPOSITE MAGAZINE

WEAR GLOBAL MAGAZINE

THE COVER

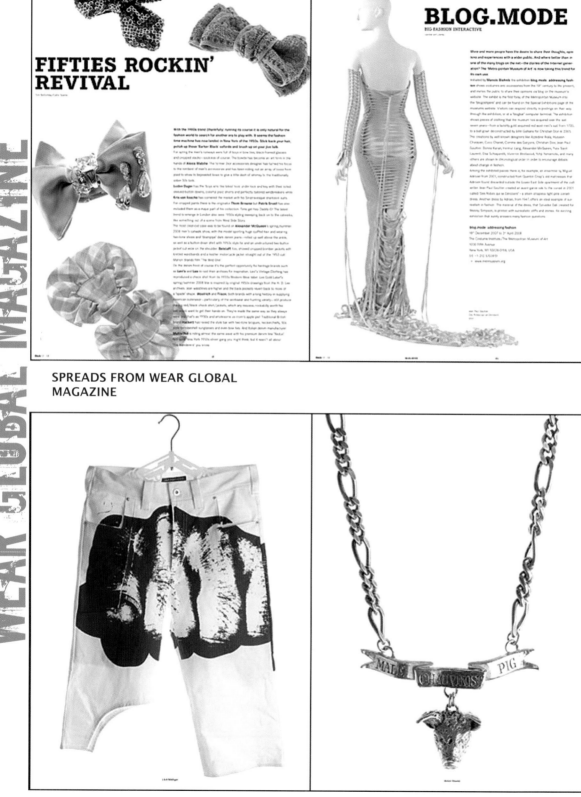

SPREADS FROM WEAR GLOBAL
MAGAZINE

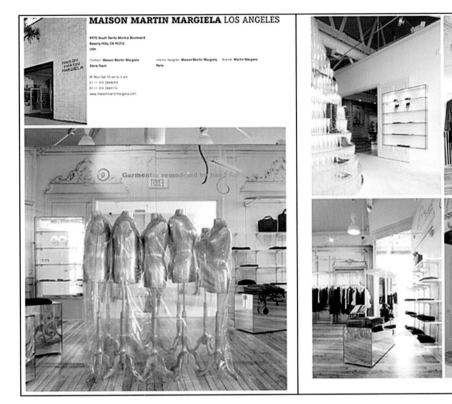

MAISON MARTIN MARGIELA LOS ANGELES

BELOW – ART BY CATALINA ESTRADA

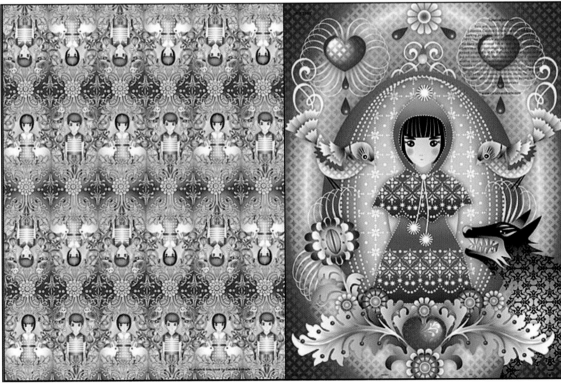

VIEW PUBLICATIONS

Part of Metropolitan Publishing BV, Amsterdam. David Shah is the publisher.
www.view-publications.com

The range of publications available are Textile View, View2, Viewpoint and Pantone View Colour Planner.

TEXTILE VIEW

Each issue of Textile View is over 300 pages long and is designed to offer information to help companies identify markets and build their fashion collections.

They have a worldwide reputation for accurate and commercial fashion prediction. Their readership extends from top end ready to wear designer names to volume distribution at High Street level.

Their target is the yarn or fabric selector or buyer and the garment/knitwear stylist and manufacturer plus major retail distributors involved in their own private label production.

Textile View covers streetwear, retail reports, men's and womenswear designer collections, haute couture, colours, accessories and trims, key shapes, casual wear, styling, forecasts and lifestyle forecasts.

VIEW2

Textile View2 is a sister publication to Textile View Magazine. It is dedicated to the world of casual, sports and jeanswear for men's, women's and childrenswear. View2 delivers practical and inspirational information to help manufacturers and retailers design, make and sell urban sports products required by the market. Its team of contributors all come from the industry with experience ranging from the latest fabric developments, through design and development, to marketing and sales.

View2 mirrors its sister publication with features dedicated to city updates, lifestyle, express fashion, current and future fashion direction.

VIEWPOINT

This is a product designed to give the reader a view of the future that will influence their design and sales strategy for tomorrow. It is necessary to know who the consumers are and what they want and expect.

It alerts decision makers, at a very early stage, to market and consumer behavioural pointers that will enable them to deliver exactly what their customers want.

PANTONE®/VIEW COLOUR PLANNER

This is a colour forecast card that is economic in cost and time. It covers fashion, cosmetics and industrial design. Colour Planner is segmented according to key colour directives.

There is a general introduction to each directive outlining the colours involved and the philosophy behind them.

These pages are followed by a more specific breakdown covering harmonies and materials according to end use. Following these key colour directives, there comes the 'basics' section breaking down the essential, commercial colours of the new season again by end use.

Colours are dyed and coded by the Pantone® colour system.

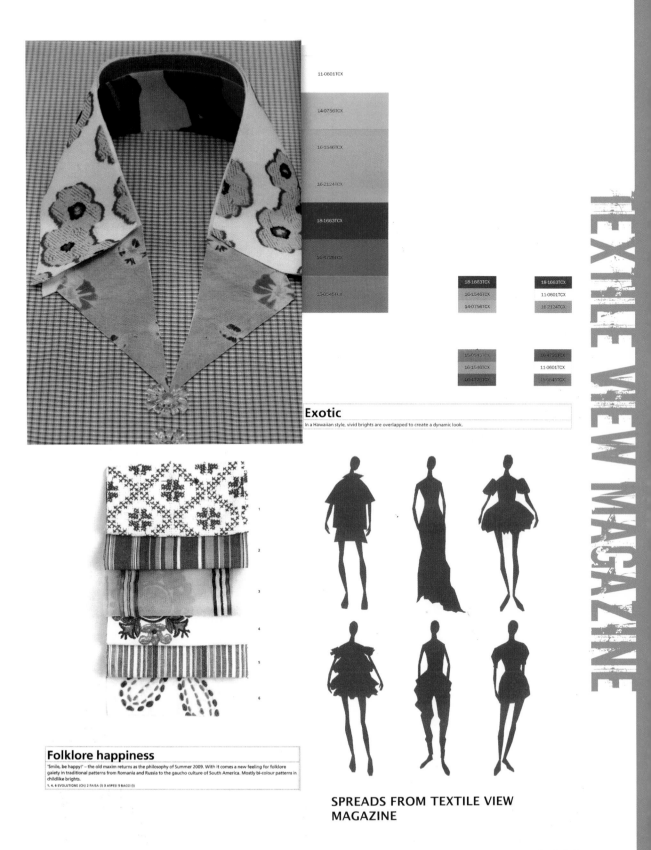

11-0601TCX

14-0756TCX

16-1546TCX

16-2124TCX

18-1663TCX

16-4725TCX

15-0545TCX

18-1663TCX		18-1663TCX
16-1546TCX		11-0601TCX
14-0756TCX		16-2124TCX

15-0545TCX		16-4725TCX
16-1546TCX		11-0601TCX
16-4725TCX		15-0545TCX

Exotic

In a Hawaiian style, vivid brights are overlapped to create a dynamic look.

Folklore happiness

'Smile, be happy!' – the old maxim returns as the philosophy of Summer 2009. With it comes a new feeling for folklore gaiety in traditional patterns from Romania and Russia to the gaucho culture of South America. Mostly bi-colour patterns in childlike brights.

1, 4, 6 EVOLUTIONE (CH) 2 FAISA (I) 3 ASPESI 5 BACCI (I)

SPREADS FROM TEXTILE VIEW MAGAZINE

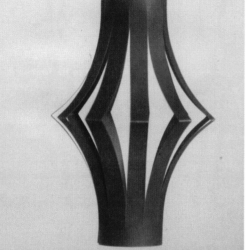

Lantern

The newest marker for the season. Narrow hemlines and tight ankles move into full volume at the hip or waist. Decidedly Middle Eastern and Eastern in influence, we will see dhoti pants, jodhpurs and lantern shaped dresses.

SPREADS FROM TEXTILE VIEW MAGAZINE

New summer boho

• multi-cultural influences • embellished details • lightweight feminine layering • pattern clashes

This story brings together an eclectic mix of influences, creating a new bohemian look for the season ahead. Cross-cultural patterns and embellishments are used to adorn a lightweight wardrobe of key summer items for the girl about town who likes to give a taste of her travelling past. Key items: patterned kaftans • relaxed pinafores • summer smocks • embellished jersey dresses. Key details: fringing and beadwork details • loose flowing silhouettes • lightweight cheesecloths • patterned borders • mini ruffles, pleats and folds.

Short and sweet

• micro hemlines • simple summer styling • tonal surface textures • oversized floral patterns

Be prepared to flash some flesh, with this young and fun women's story, where micro hemlines and wide and low necklines are key. Silhouettes can be sporty, modern and moulded or more girlie with cute ruffles, pleats and floral prints. Essentially, this is all about easy seasonal styles, designed with hot weather and the female form in mind. Key items: super short shorts • halter-neck tops • cute short sleeve jackets • simplistic shift dresses • fit and flare skirts and dresses. Key details: contrasting large trims • fitted waistlines • rounded collars • oversized pleats • deep and wide necklines.

Natural craft

Neutrals, paper shades, parchments, documents and manuscripts.
Tinted naturals. Think writing materials, books, faded quality, hemp and jute.

SPREADS FROM VIEW2 MAGAZINE

REWORKED AND REBORN

Techno-Classic

Using the best of new techniques and applying them to a wider base beyond high performance and technical end-uses for ultra functional suits, woollen coats and denim. Thermal fibres, weightless membranes, light waddings, laminates, temperature regulating pcms...It's all about the hybridisation of performance and urban wear.

1. Dondi Jersey (I)
2. Nino (D)
3. Nino (D)
4. Schoeller (CH)
5. New Cotton (I)
6. Zanotto (I)
7. Schoeller (CH)
8. Schoeller (CH)
9. Getzner (A)
10. New Cotton (I)
11. Schoeller (CH)

Protection

Highly compact structures, dense fabrics with stretch, heavily constructed weaves and exaggerated structures (the kind used for luggage and protective outfits or wrappings) in wool and synthetics. Colours reach from obvious blacks and oxidized metal hues to white and winter beige.

1. Evolutione (CH)
2. Evolutione (CH)
3. Pontetorto (I)
4. Lenzi Egisto (I)
5. Fratelli Morelli (I)
6. Zanotto (I)
7. Luigi Boggio Casero (I)
8. Hellenic (GR)

SPREADS FROM VIEW2 MAGAZINE

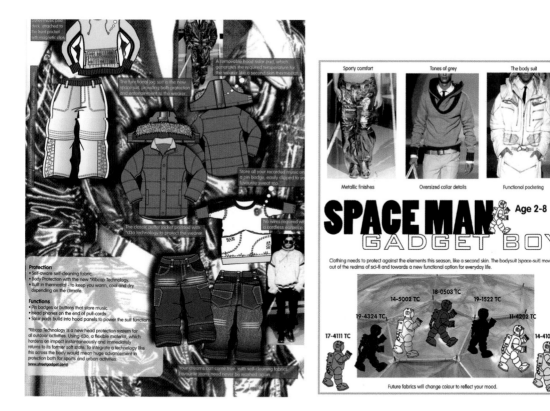

SPREADS FROM VIEW2 MAGAZINE

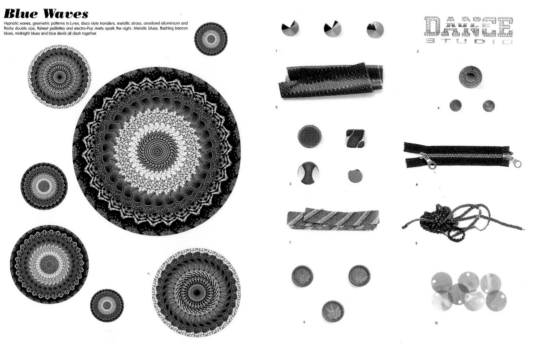

121

HocusPocus

Clockwise from left: climbing wall by Nendo, www.nendo.jp/en/; 'Divided' dressers, 'Levitating lamp and 'Vanishing' cabinet, all by Front, www.frontdesign.se; 'Sculpt' table, chair and wardrobe, by Maarten Baas, www.maartenbaas.com; 'Lathe' chair by Sebastian Brajkovic sebastianbrajkovic@hotmail.com; Etagère by Camille Debora and Gregory Pary, www.pairsdeboradesign.com; 'Basket' by Studio Job for Bisazza Home, photography by Paulo Verdant, www.studiojob.nl, www.bisazza.it

Hocus pocus, hey presto, nothing is what it seems. Super-surreal design creates a modern-day wonderland of magic and illusion. Misshapen, stretched, squashed furniture could have come through Alice's looking glass. Cabinets change their appearance, drawers and lights float in the air, the designer becomes part magician, part illusionist, wholly enchanting. Front's

collection 'Found' and 'Magic' seem to defy the laws of nature: objects disappear, levitate, balance and float. Nendo's climbing wall resembles a strange gallery where climbers grapple with empty picture frames.

Key terms: Illusion, distortion, disproportion, magic, levitation, mutation, enchantment, super-sized, surreal

TOP SPREAD FROM VIEWPOINT

BOTTOM SPREAD FROM VIEW COLOUR PLANNER

This section investigates the design process, used by the fashion forecasting industry, through exploration of each element and through a series of exercises.

It begins by looking at the first development of any season – colour. Colour is a critical element which helps to consolidate trends on the High Street. Global colour referencing is accessed through the Pantone® Colour Tool which is available to all, with many key software packages using it in their colour libraries.
A number of other supportive companies and societies are mentioned here.
A creative exercise illustrates how colour is developed for use in a new season.

The next consideration is that of inspiration, where does it come from? It is derived from exhibitions, galleries, street style, science, culture, even shop windows; with an example from the Bergdorf Goodman 'holiday' windows in New York City.
A good background knowledge about art, art movements, culture, and historical events helps in terms of reference of inspiration; this combines with the 'contemporary' to bring new fashion looks to the consumer.
Inspiration may be taken from such as the Premiere Vision fabric trade fair; here fabrics are displayed in 'stories'. The organisers also offer their own forecasts in line with other forecasting companies exhibiting at the show; this makes the fabric sourcing job much more focused for the designer.

Four fabric collections are offered that tie in with the later developed themes in this section, each fabric collection has its own inspirational roots.
Inspiration is realised through the 'Mood Board'. The initial mood board here, is a series of images with no particular 'weight' in terms of image importance. The fabric collections help to form a vision from which to develop design.

A further exercise is offered to get the most from the mood board.
Consumers today are very visually literate, here there is an opportunity for the designer to really exploit all that the mood board has to offer,   through a series of 'Seeing' exercises.
Once the mood board, colour palette, fabric story and keywords are resolved the designing may begin.

This section offers two approaches to designing – womenswear and menswear.
There are full figure illustrations showing the 'look'; these reflect the pose, attitude, silhouette, proportion, colour use and fabric use.
There are three stories for womenswear and three for menswear each depicting a different approach to a market/ consumer. The womenswear stories offer a theme on structured daywear – Order>Disorder, feminine tailoring with edgy styling to dress it down if required – Hidden>Exposed, and casual weekend wear Ordinary>Extraordinary.
The menswear stories are Kook aimed at the youth market, Busker – a slightly older male, and Taxi driver – older again.

Each story also depicts explicit black and white illustrations showing the shape, fastening, detail and finish of individual garments.
There is also a section that offers tee shirt designs developed from each of the themes/stories.
The stories are very much a shortened version of what would be offered in a traditional forecasting publication.

The menswear designs also show branding and graphics.

1.

2.

3.

COLOUR

As colour is the first development of a new season, colour stories are often expressed using whatever colour samples are available, for example, flat fabrics, yarn samples, matte ribbon. Flat, solid colour is a necessity so that there are no ambiguities in the final colour choice. This is essential when

4.   5.   6.   7.

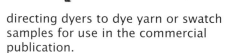

directing dyers to dye yarn or swatch samples for use in the commercial publication.

Forecasting companies like Here & There use devices such as the Color Cubicle (see the Fashion Forecasting Industry section) to display their colour stories. There is a need to accurately dye every inch of the yarn used. The background illustration shows the first thoughts for a new Spring/Summer season. Note how the seven colour palettes work tonally and show pales through brights, with midtones, to darks.

These colours would then be interpreted as Pantone® colours using a 'specifier'.

125

COLOUR TOOL – PANTONE®
www.pantone.com

Pantone®, whose headquarters are in New Jersey, USA, are the world renowned colour authority.

In the early 1960s, Lawrence Herbert, Pantone's® founder, developed a system of colour matching for the graphics industry. This system has since been expanded to work in any of the colour critical industries, such as, digital technologies, fashion, plastics, architecture, interiors, home and paint. Pantone® is known globally for its standard language for communicating colour from design to manufacture and retail to consumer.

The PANTONE FASHION & HOME® Color System is used by designers in the specification of colour used in the manufacture of textiles and fashion. The physical system consists of 1,925 colours in cotton or paper in a 'fan' booklet format, each colour has a unique identification number. These are ideal for creating and communicating colour stories.

Adobe software – InDesign, Illustrator and Photoshop – contain digital Pantone® libraries accessible through the 'Swatches' palettes.

Pantone® produce a twice yearly PANTONE VIEW® Color Planner, forecasting tool, that provides seasonal colour direction two years ahead of the season. They also produce the PANTONE SMART® Color Swatch Card System which allows designers and manufacturers to accurately speed up the colour development cycle from product development to market.
In Britain, the Society of Dyers and Colourists promotes the use of colour.

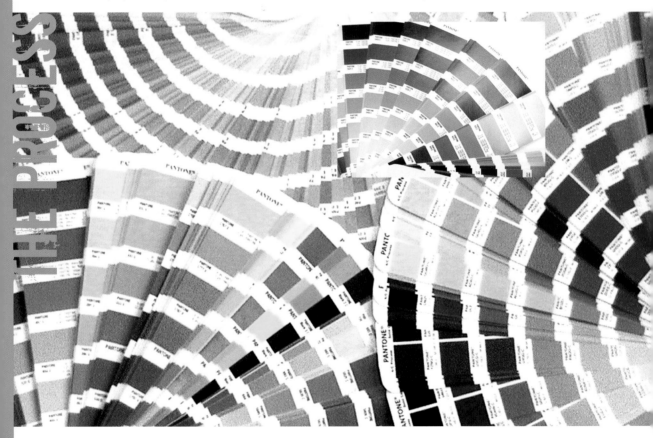

THE SOCIETY OF DYERS AND COLOURISTS
www.sdc.org.uk

The mission of the Society of Dyers and Colourists is to disseminate information throughout the colouration industry. This is achieved through the work of members of the council, through committees and membership across the world.

The society was founded in 1884 and was granted a Royal Charter of Incorporation in 1963. It is the only international professional society specialising in colour for all manner of uses. The society is based in Bradford.

Of particular interest on their website is the ColourClick tool.

The tool contains the COLOUR CENTRE: a colour showcase and colour forecast which is available to anyone that subscribes to the site.

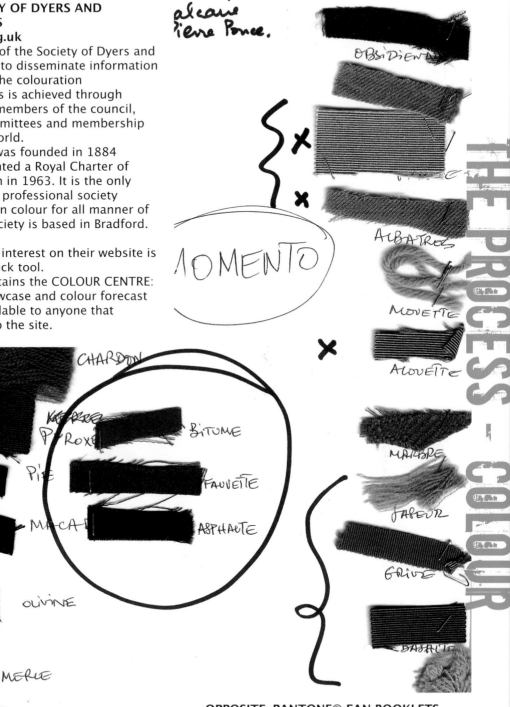

OPPOSITE, PANTONE® FAN BOOKLETS
THIS PAGE, ORGANISING AND NAMING COLOURS

127

COLOUR – DEVELOPING A PALETTE

Colour is the first to be created in a season. This is so that yarn manufacturers and suppliers may dye their yarns in the relevant colours well ahead of the selling season. Usually colour is produced up to two years ahead.

Colour palettes in forecasting, work in 'stories'. Colour palettes are inspired by exhibitions, gallery visits, interest in particular cultures, unusual imagery or historical imagery.

Here the colours selected (left at the base of the page) are pale and time worn, distressed and weathered. On closer analysis there are embossed, scratched and rubbed away surfaces. There are transparent layers (glass) with rubbed paint so there is an opportunity to peer behind the objects, there are cutouts to perform a similar 'peeking' effect, layers and worn out numbers. All of these qualities can be used to express how the colour story might be used.

One of Here & There's colour palettes is described:
"Spring Summer 2008 is a reflection on the relationship of nature and man. Nature is viewed with reverance. The wholesome values and everyday poetry of rural settings finds a new urban audience...Whitened neutrals are essential, along with organic herbal tones. The contrast of vivid colours and neutrals is very important, as 60's influence pairs joyous brights and plastic pastels with Mod white."

Their colour stories for this season were:
Romanticist – White Washes, Dry Roses, Petal Lights.
Modernist – Translucent Pop, Vivid Synthetics, Standard Brights.
Naturalist – Vegetable Dyes, Organic Minerals, Exclusive Darks.
Formalist – Standard Brights with Industrial Darks plus White.

Opposite is a strip of colour representing the proportion of colour as analysed from these visuals; this is done by eye, and allows thought as to how the colour might be used, for example, as base colours and accents or stripings and geometric patterns.

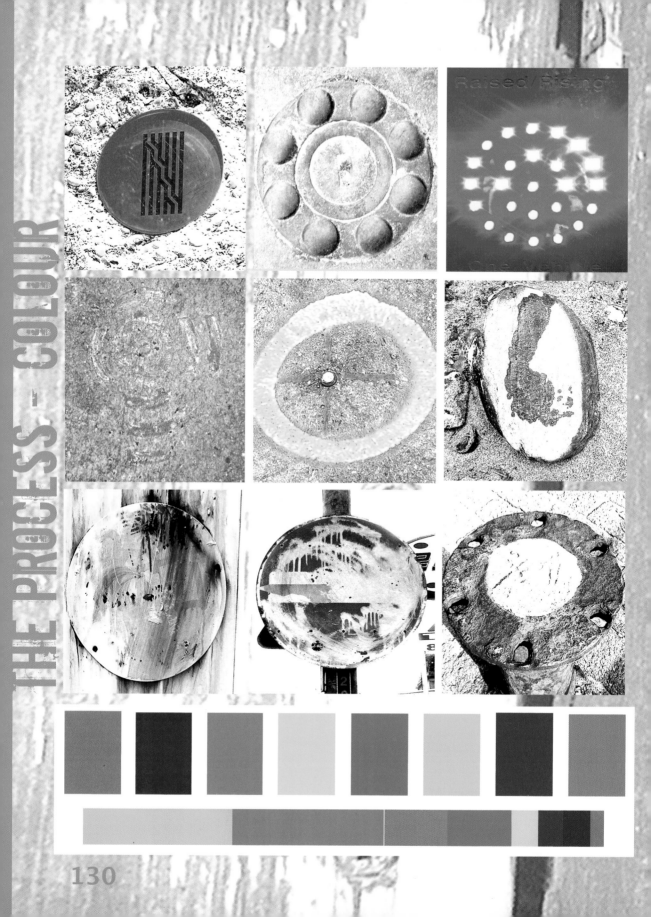

These were photographs taken from around the world, with a 'feeling' for 'circles'. The photographs were originally slightly overexposed so required some colour adjustment in Adobe Photoshop.

This was achieved by opening all of the images in Photoshop and then going to Image>Adjustments>Brightness/Contrast.

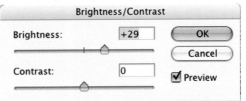

This creates a pop up box which allows either Brightness or Contrast, or both to be manipulated. The tools in the menu above are invaluable when adjusting colour.

This page shows the development of a midtone colour story. The theme of circles connects the visuals together and 'brights' are the common colours.

NB: When working with colour, the stories should be displayed on a white background, to avoid pollution from surrounding colour.

DAWN – PALES

MIDDAY – BRIGHTS

MIDNIGHT – DARKS

Most colour stories may require another story or two to work with, for example, Here & There suggested for the Romanticist story that 'White Washes' could combine with 'Dry Roses' for feminine, country charm or sweeten with 'Petal Lights' for youthful naivety. The Modernist story could work 'Translucent Pop' with 'Vivid Synthetics' for cheery optimism or pair 'Vivid Synthetics' with 'Standard Brights' for rich vivacity. Merge 'Vegetable Dyes' with 'Organic Minerals' for masculine rusticity or combine 'Organic Minerals' with 'Exclusive Darks' for lavish depth. Expressing stories like this helps to establish ideas for which story is relevant to which market or for the use of fabrics and silhouettes.

CREATING A COLOUR PALETTE DIGITALLY

Once the images are captured by camera and downloaded, or scanned in, it is possible to create the palette by using Adobe InDesign (see the final part of the book for more information on using this software).

Make a new document in InDesign, make a series of boxes with the Rectangle Frame Tool, select one of the boxes by clicking into it then go to File>Place and select an inspirational image, this will appear in the layout, use Object>Fitting and make a choice of how you want to display the image, make more smaller boxes to use as the colour palette then keep one selected, go to the Eyedropper Tool and place it onto the image to pick up a colour. The colour will appear in the selected box. Continue until you have created the story.

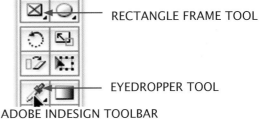

RECTANGLE FRAME TOOL

EYEDROPPER TOOL

ADOBE INDESIGN TOOLBAR

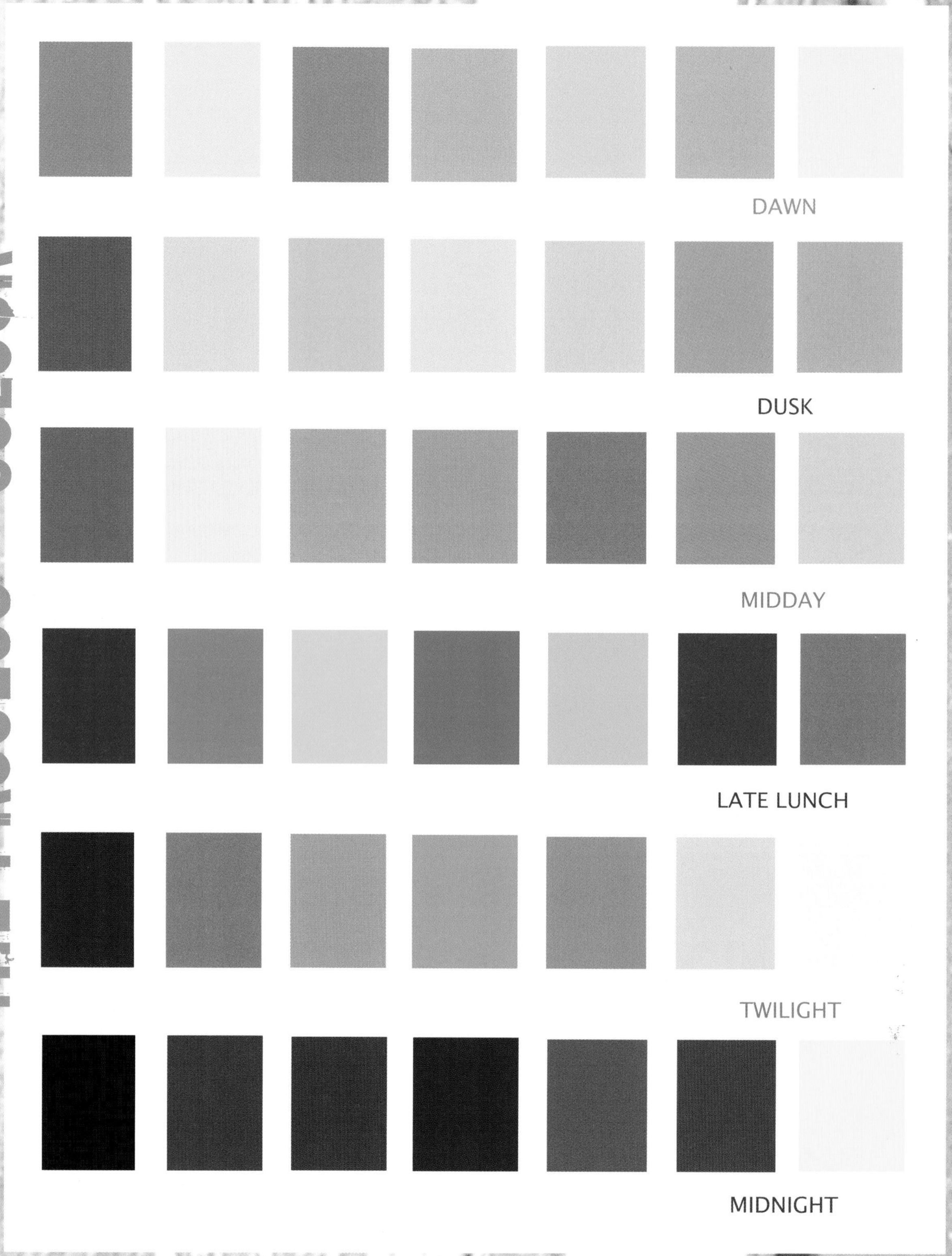

DAWN

DUSK

MIDDAY

LATE LUNCH

TWILIGHT

MIDNIGHT

Forecasting companies often provide the facility to manipulate the colour. Here & There use the yarns in the Color Cubicle so that clients can cut and create colour combinations of their own (see Here & There in the first section). Using a metaphor across all of the stories – here the times of day – can help to unify the stories for a season. It also helps to explain that the colours often work in tones and depth of colour, pales (DAWN), midtones (MIDDAY), and darks (MIDNIGHT) with ranges inbetween. MIDNIGHT is inspired by street art shot in the dark, hence its grainy, more sinister inspiration and would link with TWILIGHT as a theme for design, but not necessarily as colour stories.

The combinations here are quite ad hoc, but often stories will be mixed deliberately, for example, MIDDAY could be mixed tonally with DUSK. DUSK could be used as a more romantic base colour with MIDDAY as accent colours in prints. MIDNIGHT and DUSK could also work together tonally for a more dramatic layered look. DAWN is pale and could also work with MIDNIGHT as a complete contrast, but DAWN is not a timid range as its inspiration comes from old, rusty, utilitarian objects (see previous pages). TWILIGHT stands alone because of the autumnal quality of its colour, but it is not autumnal in its inspiration; it is derived from the 'Contextual Art' inspiration and should be used in this streetwise way to give it 'edge'. The stronger colours would be used in small amounts on washed out, painterly or concrete-like backgrounds.

These stories have a washed out effect, some with slightly dirty tones as if they were tainted in the wash. Some colours are too close to each other and require modifying but consider this a confirmation of direction. Naming the stories can be evocative and expressive for designing, for example, Here & There's Summer pales – White Washes, Dry Roses and Petal Lights are allied to the Romanticism theme.

INSPIRATION

A key element of any new season is what inspires that season. In a visually rich world there is a constant need to keep stimulating the fashion consumer be it through mood, print, pattern, texture. Visual inspiration comes from such sources as, exhibitions, galleries, artists shows and retrospectives, science, magazines, innovative design and architecture.

INSPIRATION – CONTEXTUAL ART

Fashion requires the 'fresh' to inspire design and offer something new to the customer.

The imagery on this spread was gathered from New York and Paris and requires the intelligence gatherer to carry a camera at all times.

This exercise resulted in finding imagery that forms an 'art-like' appearance because of the context of where and when it was found. Also the camera allows the viewer to edit and crop the art even more and, like much street art, artists add their own efforts to others. The overall effect is due to the wall surface and its aged properties, torn elements carried out by others which add a distressed effect.

Capturing a 'moment in time' is also part of the joy of gathering unique imagery, for example, in the sticker art immediately to the left, the two human figures work as a pair (paired by the author not the artists). The colour and utilitarian workman elements add to the imagery, but much more fun is the idea of catching the armoured figure as if he is climbing the transiently placed ladders the wrong way and the other figure descending from above, a surreal image captured in New York City.

This type of imagery could inspire colour palettes, surface textures, print and graphic ideas.

When imagery is organised and themes are repeated such as shapes, feelings and colour, across the world, then a trend may well develop and be considered a 'direction'.

137

INSPIRATION – BERGDORF GOODMAN WINDOWS

A regular supply of rich and decorative inspiration is the world famous Bergdorf Goodman department store on 5th Avenue in New York City.
In the 'holiday' period, Christmas vacation 2006 in this instance, they dressed their windows with particular themes in mind. The photographs displayed on the two following spreads captured the following themes: Astound, Decorate, Entertain, Recollect, Cultivate, Wonder all presented as if they were part of a circus show.

The windows for Christmas 2007 were described on the Bergdorf Goodman website under the heading UNVEILED (www.bergdorfgoodman.com/store): "Gaze into the elemental worlds of our holiday window displays. Decorated in the 'natural baroque' style of Tony Duquette, these lush dreamworlds abound in avant–garde elegance, rococo ornamentation and a warm golden glow.

Discover all we have to offer."

Tony Duquette was a cultural 'American Design icon', a native of Los Angeles, California and internationally acclaimed artist and designer, popular from the 1940s.

Bergdorf Goodman set their contemporary fashion collections in amongst these very decorative 'themed' surroundings.

Acquiring knowledge about different art movements, cultures and design icons is useful to the intelligence gatherer who may need to draw upon their knowledge in any season.

The visuals illustrated here offered a richness in theme and texture that called upon a variety of media and knowledge to display.
The windows were constantly photographed by designers and tourists alike during their short life.

DECORATE

BERGDORF GOODMAN WINDOW
DISPLAYS

Fashion Forecasting companies attend all of the major fabric and yarn trade fairs.

Premiere Vision is probably the best known fabric trade fair in the world. It shows in September (Autumn/Winter season) and February (Spring/Summer season) of any given year. Premiere Vision also hold shows in New York, Moscow, Shanghai and Tokyo.

PREMIERE VISION

It is held at the Parc d'Exposition de Paris-Nord Villepinte. Four trade shows combine where 50,000 fashion professionals from 110 countries congregate to conduct business, build collections and exchange ideas. Four major shows exhibit at the same time:

PREMIERE VISION – Colours and fabrics are displayed 18 months in advance of the season.
www.premierevision.fr

EXPOFIL – Yarns and fibres.
www.expofil.com

LE CUIR A PARIS – Leather, fur, textiles, shoes, leather goods, clothing, furnishing and car interiors.
www.lecuiraparis.com

INDIGO
Designers, from all over the world, show their textile designs, including a 'new technologies' area.
www.indigo-salon.com
This combination of trade fairs show under the brand name of Premiere Vision.

An 'International Concertation' brings weavers spokesmen and forecasting companies together, well before each trade fair, to exchange ideas about significant trends for the coming season including colour and fibre trends. This information is exclusively previewed by the exhibitors who then make the most of the information to provide strong direction at the show.

A few weeks before the trade fairs occur, another meeting consolidates the main directions which are shown as audio-visual presentations and films, fashion seminars, colour stories, fabric information and catalogues.
The 'mantra' of these shows is:
"To choose a colour for its strength, an idea for its meaning and a fabric for its fibre."

During the show's four days of exposure, Premiere Vision produces a newspaper which features daily reports, interviews with buyers and weavers and any other items of interest.

There are many other professional textile bodies available for support and information around the world, most accessible online, at any time. Three key players in the textile industry are Cotton Incorporated, Lycra.com and The Woolmark Company.
Each of these bodies provides colour and trends services to promote their products in a competitive marketplace. Most of these services are free to, or require nominal fees from, subscribers of the bodies.

COTTON INCORPORATED
www.cottoninc.com
This group's remit is to visit cotton producing textile mills and keep in touch with manufacturers and product sourcers. It strives to support the development of the best cotton products possible and aims to help to develop supply and sourcing relationships and other meaningful contacts globally.
It has a range of resources at the disposal of industry contacts with a view to using cotton more effectively.
The resources are:
TECHNICAL SERVICES – including fibre processing, product development, dyeing and finishing and cotton quality management assistance.
THE COTTONWORKS® Global Fabric Library is also available and is a searchable online directory with details

on woven, knits, home furnishing, lace/trim constructions that contain 100% cotton or are cotton rich (60% or more cotton content).

INFORMATION SERVICES – provide information on cotton supply/demand, fibre quality and consumer research trends. Many of these services are available on the website. They are delivered as multi-media seminars and one-on-one presentations.

PRODUCT TREND ANALYSIS SERVICES – these are intended to maintain cotton's position in the world of fashion, to keep cotton uppermost in the minds of those who will forecast fabric use. These services are achieved through presentations with designers and specialists highlighting the group's trend research and supplier information.

THE WOOLMARK COMPANY
www.wool.com

This company specialises in the commercialisation of wool innovations and technologies, technical consultation, business information and the commercial testing of wool fabrics. They own the WOOLMARK, WOOLMARK BLEND and WOOL BLEND license and provide global quality endorsement. The brands and symbols are protected by extensive control checks and are recognised globally as signs of quality.

The company works with textile processors, designers and retailers in fashion, apparel and interior textile markets worldwide.

The company has been generating colour for the wool industry for over 30 years. Woolmark Colour Trends are designed to support the need to evolve the natural animal hair fibre business. Their shades are provided to the International Dyestuff manufacturers guidelines. They also provide a Pantone® Textile colour reference for each seasonal colour. They offer reports on Apparel and Interior Colour Trends. Woolmark Market Intelligence also provides global market intelligence developed from a comprehensive

statistical database on the wool sector.

LYCRA.COM
www.lycra.com

Today, Lycra®, the stretch fibre, may be found in almost any garment made from natural and man-made fibres from denim, leather, silk and cotton. The Lycra® brand is considered, by the company INVISTA, to be an evolving fashion icon with an unrivalled position in the apparel industry.

According to the website:

"INVISTA and the Lycra® brand are a vital source for both trends and innovations for the fashion fraternity worldwide always at the vanguard of the latest fabric developments, trend forecasts and fashion presentations. INVISTA is committed to innovation and the Lycra® brand will continue to meet the demands of the world's designers, giving ever greater comfort, fit and freedom of movement to clothing."

The fabrics displayed on the following two spreads are from textile collections by final year students on the BA (Hons) Fashion degree at Northumbria University. These students are studying on the Textile option.

The structural, geometric designs, on this page, use cut-outs, surface textures and print and are by Judith Bull.

The collections have been selected because of their relationship to the story boards being developed as a womenswear case study, in this section. However, each collection was researched and developed using different sources. The fact that the collections relate to the womenswear case study is testament to the idea that disparate cultural threads and intuition play a part in forecasting; it is the intelligence gatherer that pulls together the threads and makes sense of them.

These embroideries, couching and discharge prints are by Julie Mills.

145

THE PROCESS – FABRICS

These embroideries, figurative and abstract designs are by Laura Armstrong.

146

These embroideries, surface cut-outs and repeat prints are by Sarah Kennedy.

To illustrate the synthesis of the process, two case studies have been developed, one in womenswear, the other in menswear. The first will show three womenswear themes for a Spring/ Summer season. The second will show three menswear themes for a Spring/ Summer season.

MOOD BOARD DESIGN

Here the mood boards and colour stories for the womenswear themes are developing; images with resonance and colour similarity are pulled together, key descriptive words are defined; the fabric story is developing also with reference to the fashion student textile collections and with the addition of basic fabrics also. The story boards indicate three different directions and potential markets.

They all come together as the ingredients for the new moods for the season.

This is the application of a normal fashion design process (see Fashion Design: Process, Innovation and Practice published by Wiley-Blackwell).

INITIAL KEYWORDS:
Order>Disorder
Underlying Structure, Boarding, Weathered Structure Textured Background, Door in Cliff, Floor Numbers, Graffiti Letters, Corner Positioning (Graffiti), Small Windows, Boarded up Window, Prominent, Grouped in Threes, Inside View, Stripped Wallpaper, Stained Wallpaper, Rough Background.

Hidden>Exposed
Layered Type, Decorative, Uppercase, Formal Font Late 19th Century, Cut-outs, Revealing, Distressed Painted Glass, Scratched, Transparent, Formal, Numbers, Precious, Stone, Fragile, Porcelain – Outside Ornaments, From Inside-out.

Ordinary>Extraordinary
Two Friendly Flies, Spray Painted Chain, Imprint, Stud in Centre of Target, Hand Painted Numbers Utility Paint – Utilitarian, Scale – Blow-up, Stickers – Price Tickets, Stencils, Street Art, Symbols/Icons, Embossed Surface, Raised Surfaces, Shoeprint, Sandy Texture, Scratched/Naïve.

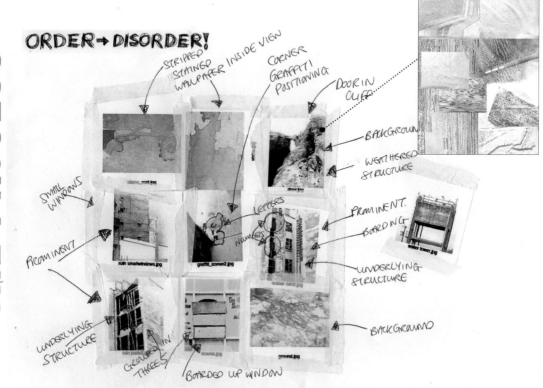

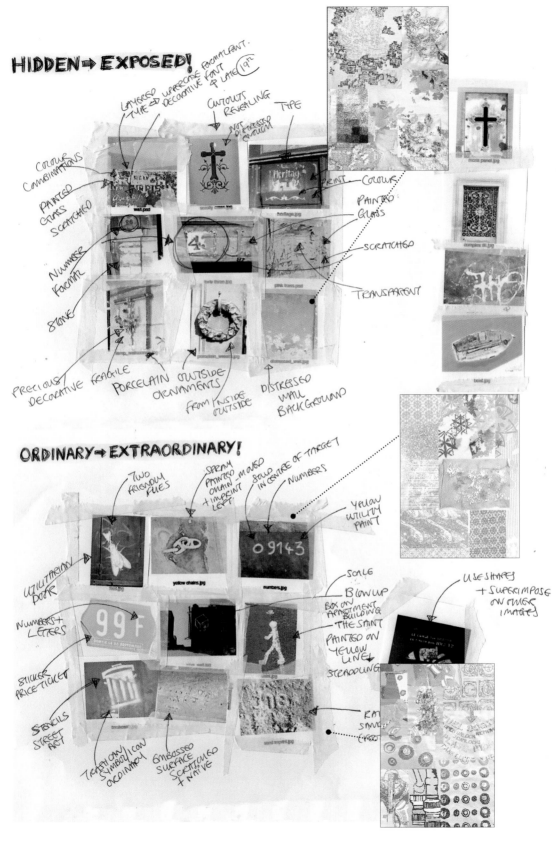

HIDDEN → EXPOSED!

ORDINARY → EXTRAORDINARY!

WHAT IS A MOOD BOARD?

Mood boards are usually a collection of images, texture, colour etc., compiled with the intention of communicating a visual statement. Provoking a mood to inspire designers, which words alone cannot achieve.

There follow a series of exercises to 'analyse' and 'explore' mood boards. It can be hard at first, for design students to understand how to 'analyse' and 'explore' visual statements in mood boards. Experienced fashion designers are able to 'analyse' a visual statement and 'explore' their own interpretation, which is then applied to their design.

The exercises which follow reveal how experienced fashion designers 'analyse' and 'explore' the mood board, using the 'example mood board' on page 162. The exercises can be carried out separately, however more value can be gained from going through each exercise in turn. It may be an idea during these exercises, to take a break now and then, because designers can become fascinated with the detail, stopping them from seeing the bigger picture.

After you have gone through the exercise, there are mood boards for you to try out the exercises yourself on pages 158, 162 and 166.

'ANALYSING' EXERCISE 1: TAKING TIME TO LOOK

Understanding a mood board takes time, there is no specific way of looking. This exercise intends to open your eyes to what you are seeing, by taking time to look at the mood board on page 162, through the following steps:

Examples for each step are placed below using the 'example mood board' on page 162.

STEP 1

Place the selected mood board at a distance so that you see the whole page. Then explore the mood board for 5 minutes. Question the unfamiliar, let questions emerge about what you are seeing, bearing in mind there are no wrong or right answers when reading a mood board.
Make some notes during this process.

How do the flowers contrast with the traditional look?

Why are traditional fonts used?

Why are some of the images distressed?

Where would I see these images?

Why is there stone and wood used in the mood board?

STEP 2

Take a break for a few minutes and then come back. This will allow you to see more in the mood board.

Why are the flowers static? Do they have a hidden message?

Why am I getting the feeling of being in a church?

What type of candle is used in the mood board?

What is the meaning of the word 'heritage' in the mood board?

'ANALYSING' EXERCISE 2: UNDERSTANDING THE VISUAL STATEMENT

The previous exercise allowed you time to open your eyes to what you are seeing. The next step involves analysing the visual statement, in the mood board, in greater depth. The point of this exercise is to develop the ability to analyse a visual statement.

You can analyse visual statements from many viewpoints (which is covered later on in this exercise). One of the most enlightening approaches is to break down the visual elements in turn, to understand how each element contributes to the whole picture.
The following steps take you through this process:

STEP 1

Select keywords to describe how the mood board makes you feel.
Then consider where in the mood board the feeling comes from.

Feeling	Where
Still in time	Flowers/candle
On edge	Distressed images
There is an untold story	Distressed images/ traditional fonts
Loneliness/ sadness	Open space

STEP 2

Visual elements are the building blocks of the visual statement, they are not to be mixed up with the medium – paint, drawing etc. Each of the following visual elements explains a different part of the visual statement:

a. Colour is the most emotive element, it is loaded with information. Colours can be associated with culture or region, they can also have symbolic meaning. Think of the colour RED: in Europe red means danger (stop signs), in China red is a sign of good luck. Colour can be assumed without actually showing the colour, for example think of a black and white picture of a person looking angry, it can convey the colour red.

Colour	Association/ Cultural
Yellow	Caution, decay
Pink	Love, girls/ Wedding, friendship
Green	Growth, fresh Islamic
Blue	Knowledge

b. Texture appeals to another sense – touch. It allows you to feel with your eyes, it enriches our own experience.

Distress, etching, dirty. Don't want to touch it, want to stand back and look at it.

'ANALYSING' EXERCISE 2:
UNDERSTANDING THE VISUAL
STATEMENT (continued)

c. Shapes can be organic and geometric.

Organic shapes are naturally
occurring, free flowing and have an
irregular outline.

Geometric shapes are regular and
predictable, each of which conveys their
own characteristic.
Circles evoke warmth, triangles stand
for action and squares are considered
honest.

There is a mixture of organic and
geometric shapes. The natural shape of
the flowers portrays warmth.

The building and typeface are geometric
shapes portraying a traditional feel.

d. Scale works with other visual
elements, it places emphasis on the page
in relationship to other objects but also
in relation to their environment.

e. Line shows movement and speed to
convey a feeling, for example, which of
the signatures below conveys freedom,
or fear? Which signature took more time
to write?

The flowers are not life-size, in
comparison to the background
man-made image.

The line scratched into the top image,
shows confidence.

'ANALYSING' EXERCISE 2:
UNDERSTANDING THE VISUAL
STATEMENT (continued)

STEP 3
Consider other elements that influence
the visual message.

a. Images can be symbolic representa-
tions, for example, the dove is a
Christian symbol of peace and purity.

b. Understanding the cultural, social,
historical and political contexts can inform the visual statement.
Take this cultural example, is this a male
or female toilet sign?

The meaning of this sign changes when
you see both of the toilet signs on the
next page and understand that the
picture was taken in South Africa, in a
bushman museum.
If an image in the mood board appears
unfamiliar it is important to ask the
question 'does it have any cultural/
social/political/historical significance?'.

Symbolism	Association
Flower	The Victorians have a language of flowers (to express feeling).
Anemone flowers	Greek word for wind; the wind blows the petals open.
Knot of flowers Known as 'Tussie-mus-ies' (posy)	Used to convey secret messages in Victorian times between lover and friend.

Cultural Association
The flower's meaning, candle and
traditional font, point to the Victorian era
(1987–1901).

Political Association
In the Victorian age, women's rights were
changed, under the Married Women's
Property Act 1882. The Act ensured that
married women had the same rights to
buy, sell and own property as unmarried
women did, which changed how the
mood board was viewed.

'ANALYSING' EXERCISE 2:
UNDERSTANDING THE VISUAL
STATEMENT (continued)

STEP 4
Now have a break, before coming back to describe the visual statement.

STEP 5
To describe the visual statement, review the relationship between the elements.

As mentioned above there are different ways to 'analyse' a visual statement. How an image is analysed depends on a person's values and beliefs, influencing their 'way of seeing'.

For example, if we think of a police investigator: the job requires them to select a method, which would be appropriate to solve the problem. They would review the above visual elements and factors and implement them in a creative way.
Whereas, if you think about a priest, although the priest respects other peoples viewpoints, the priest believes through the writings of the Bible.
The priest's frame of reference would be influenced by religious symbolism.

You have to become aware of how your values and beliefs influence how you analyse the visual statement.

Visual statement:
The visual statement, in the mood board, is indicative of the Victorian era, because the images of flowers and candle relate to the changing role of women during this time period and how they used hidden messages communicated through the flowers. The distressed textures and lines make you look again at the visual statement, to understand and explore the time period in more depth.

Keywords:

Victorian

Women

Hidden messages

'EXPLORING' EXERCISE 1: FINDING A FOCUS TO EXPLORE

Use the following questions to aid you in finding a focus to explore, based on your analysis in the previous exercise:

Examples of each step are placed below:

STEP 1

Go back to something in the mood board which surprised, interests and puzzles you. It could be an emotion that you felt, a visual element, or a factor, which influenced the visual statement.

"VICTORIAN HERITAGE"

The focus is 'Victorian Heritage'

STEP 2

Look across the mood board, decide on a focus, give it a name and summarise your interest in a sentence.

Why: This focus develops on the Victorian era, the traditional decor style and the role of women.

'EXPLORING' EXERCISE 2: EXPLORING A FOCUS

Mind maps use word, image, colour and material, to aid a person in exploring ideas freely.

This exercise intends to use mind mapping to explore further direction of research and develop your focus through the following steps:

STEP 1

To explore your focus you will need a range of different materials, a large piece of paper.

The full mind mapping example can be found on the next page.

STEP 2

Place your focus in the middle of the page. Before mapping research the following areas:

Physical objects, time period(s), events, lifestyle, fashion, visual styles, artists, transport associated with your focus. What comes before and after the time period? Consider other questions to explore.

The image below shows close-ups of the mind map, displaying the area regarding 'physical object' and 'time period'.

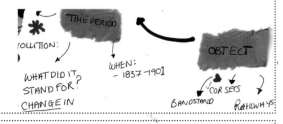

STEP 3

Then mind map the areas on the large sheet of paper.

STEP 4

Now step back from your mind map, have a break and then come back to group the mind map in the areas below:

Social: Lifestyle, meeting place, common interests, demographics, religion, shopping.
Historical: Time periods. Cultural–Visual style, colour, music, film, television, art.
Political: Government acts, ethical, equality, war.

The mind map has highlighted social, historical, cultural and political areas using the key below.

SOCIAL
HISTORICAL
CULTURAL
POLITICAL

THE FULL MIND MAP

'EXPLORING' EXERCISE 3: EXPLORING A FOCUS WITH OTHERS

Until this point the visual judgements have been made based on your own experience – your age, culture and education. It is necessary to explore and develop on your focus with peers, however conversations with peers do not come naturally, but can be fostered through the steps below:

STEP 1
Before asking a peer(s) to explore your focus. You should be able to describe your focus:
a. Describe what you did to 'analyse' the visual statement.
b. Describe the thinking behind your focus:
    Why did you select this focus?
    What did you gain from the exercise carried out with the mind map?
c. Consider any question you may have to ask your peer(s)?

STEP 2
Start by explaining what you did and the thinking behind your focus, using your mind map to help the conversation. Ask your peer or tutor to tick areas of interest on your mind map and comment on areas which can be expanded.

STEP 3
After the conversation with your peer, consider the following questions:
a. What areas were the focus of the conversation?
b. What areas were not discussed?
c. What new ideas have you gained? What new areas can be explored, which then can be added to the mind map?

STEP 4
After you have updated your mind map, stand back and look at the big picture; what do you now see?

Opposite, on the right, is the mood board that was analysed. There follows an exercise illustrating how each mood board was developed using fabric stories, colour, silhouette and detail. Designer collections would also be referred to for directional silhouettes.

Examples from **STEP 2** are placed below:

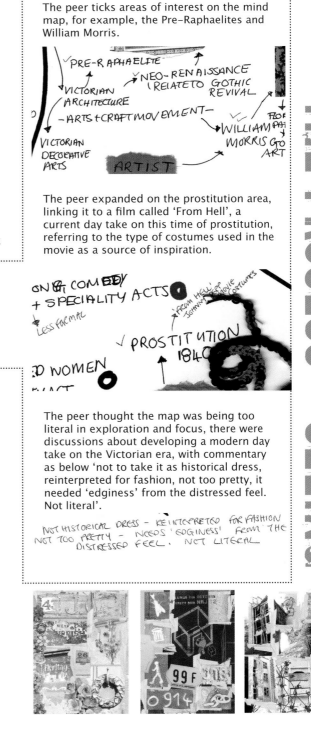

The peer ticks areas of interest on the mind map, for example, the Pre-Raphaelites and William Morris.

The peer expanded on the prostitution area, linking it to a film called 'From Hell', a current day take on this time of prostitution, referring to the type of costumes used in the movie as a source of inspiration.

The peer thought the map was being too literal in exploration and focus, there were discussions about developing a modern day take on the Victorian era, with commentary as below 'not to take it as historical dress, reinterpreted for fashion, not too pretty, it needed 'edginess' from the distressed feel. Not literal'.

157

ORDER>DISORDER

Underlying Structure, Boarding, Weathered Structure, Textured Background, Door in Cliff, Floor Numbers, Graffiti Letters – Corner Positioning, Small Windows, Boarded up Window, Prominent, Grouped in Threes, Inside View, Stripped Wallpaper, Stained Wallpaper, Rough Background.

This section shows how all of the design elements are synthesised together, the colour, inspiration, fabric story, full figure silhouette, garment outline drawings/flats and tee shirt graphics.

Forecasting services provide a number of
fashion stories for a new season. This case
study offers three variations for Spring/Sum–
mer. Each variation aims to offer ideas for
a different market, appealing to a range of
consumers. However, there is often a broad
theme crossing over each story. Here the
similarity is that of buildings, being
demolished, being painted upon and of old
traditional, distressed buildings.

Black and white drawings of 'flats'
explain more about the detail and shape of
the story's garments. They show drape and
hang. They may also show print placement or
the use of mixed fabrics within a garment.
Adobe Illustrator was used to create the
drawings.
Tee shirt ideas, for each theme, are also
offered by many forecasting services –
opposite.

160

Order>Disorder
The silhouette is boxy and structured, stripped back, high waisted and held in position by straps and belts echoing the dilapidated buildings being boarded up. Prints add interest but are mainly in the accessories and tee shirts, fabric surfaces are structured, textural and coarse like the buildings.

161

HIDDEN>EXPOSED

Layered Type, Decorative, Uppercase, Formal Font Late
19th Century, Cut-outs, Revealing, Distressed
Painted Glass, Scratched, Transparent, Formal, Numbers,
Precious, Stone, Fragile, Porcelain – Outside Ornaments,
From Inside-out.

The mood board pulls together a range of
images from which a colour story is derived.
The fabric stories are related to the mood
board and keywords are used to describe the
attitude and potential structure of the
clothing. This mood board was the subject of
the analysis in the 'Seeing' exercise.

The pose and styling attempts to illustrate the targeted market, the age, hairstyle and attitude of the consumer. 'Lifestyle' is loosely evoked in the context of the illustration.

163

Hidden > Exposed

The silhouette is tailored and formal in layers inspired by old and traditional buildings with surfaces scratched away revealing another age. Garments are heavily embroidered or printed in a faded, time worn colour palette.

The look could be styled up with heels or down with sports shoes. Ornamentation is from the inside taken outside.
Tee shirt designs are feminine shapes with exaggerated prints.

ORDINARY>EXTRAORDINARY

KEYWORDS
Two Friendly Flies, Spray Painted Chain, Imprint, Stud in Centre of Target, Hand Painted Numbers, Utility Paint – Utilitarian, Scale – Blow-up, Stickers – Price Tickets, Stencils, Street Art, Symbols/Icons, Embossed Surface, Raised Surfaces, Shoeprint, Sandy Texture, Scratched/Naïve.

Ordinary>Extraordinary
The silhouette is drapy and relaxed, layered in an informal way. The look is practical and comfortable in a utilitarian colour palette. The surfaces are inspired by urban buildings with stencilled surfaces. Repetitive geometric patterns and the ordinary world around us also inspires prints. Prints vary in scale from the tiny repeat to the enormous placed print.

166

167

Shape direction is taken from the designer collections and through intuition of what may happen next (intuition is based on experience of the cyclical nature of fashion); drape and hang reflects the lifestyle element of the theme, for example, soft layers are relaxed, structured tailoring is more formal.

THE PROCESS – CASE STUDY MENSWEAR

Research is a process of seeking and recording creative information in order to compile a bank of visual information for inspirational purposes. It is essential, in the forecasting process, as an intelligence gathering technique and is primarily an investigation of what instinctively feels new, fresh and exciting, a documented observation of contemporary visual images and current cultural influences.

The process of recording research material provides a focus from which to start generating ideas, which can come from anywhere; they can be completely original and be only connected to the designer in a very individualistic way. Or, they can be influenced by the current zeitgeist, being part of ongoing trends. The sources of inspiration are individual and related to the designer's personal experience.

Research can be divided into two types: investigative research which involves seeking and recording information from a wide range of reference points, for example, historical sources, museums, exhibitions, shops and collecting materials, photographing details of construction techniques, exploring a specific area in depth. The second is inspirational; this can be drawn or photographed from any source and is often a wide ranging selection of images, materials, colour schemes, articles, sketches, fabrics, notes, scraps of wrapping paper, wallpaper, advertisements, photographs, trimmings, articles, sewn samples, memorabilia, postcards, old patterns, video, animation clips, music and graphics, anything that is aesthetically and thematically inspiring.

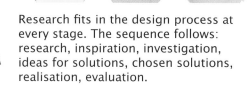

Research fits in the design process at every stage. The sequence follows: research, inspiration, investigation, ideas for solutions, chosen solutions, realisation, evaluation.

THE PROCESS – CASE STUDY MENSWEAR

The three menswear themes on the following pages were created from photographs taken in Paris in September 2007; they were separated into three themes by colour and mood and a colour story was derived from each. The themes were kept deliberately close in style, all being variations on men's casual wear; the first theme is aimed at a relatively young market, the second and third progressively older.

MOOD AND COLOUR

The first double page spread of colour and images suggests the theme title and background ideas for decorative and graphic treatments and effects. A mood board of visual images sets the scene for the colour palette, product and fabrication; it allows the designer to see the texture and patina of the colours and visualise decorative effects. There is a strong feeling for the profile of the market, age and attitude of the target customer. This is often accompanied by descriptive text.

FABRICATION AND SILHOUETTE

The second double page spread illustrates the look, attitude, styling and types of fabrics suggested. The colour palette is expanded into fabrication, finish, texture, pattern, handle and decoration. The proportion and balance of colour, pattern and texture is illustrated indicating silhouette.

DETAIL

The third double page spread illustrates, in black and white, a hypothetical capsule collection suggesting cut, construction, trimming, detail and decorative effects; these are often produced as black and white images for clarity.

GRAPHICS AND LABELLING

The fourth double page spread shows ideas for promotional graphics, labelling, swing tags and zip pulls for each theme, illustrating a variety of ways in which a brand can be reinforced through garment embellishment. Graphic images are used to suggest ideas for other product areas, like T–shirts; these are not always intended to be used literally, rather as a vehicle to initiate the design thinking process.

PARIS
A/W 07/08
MENSWEAR

Kook

busker

TAXI
DRIVER

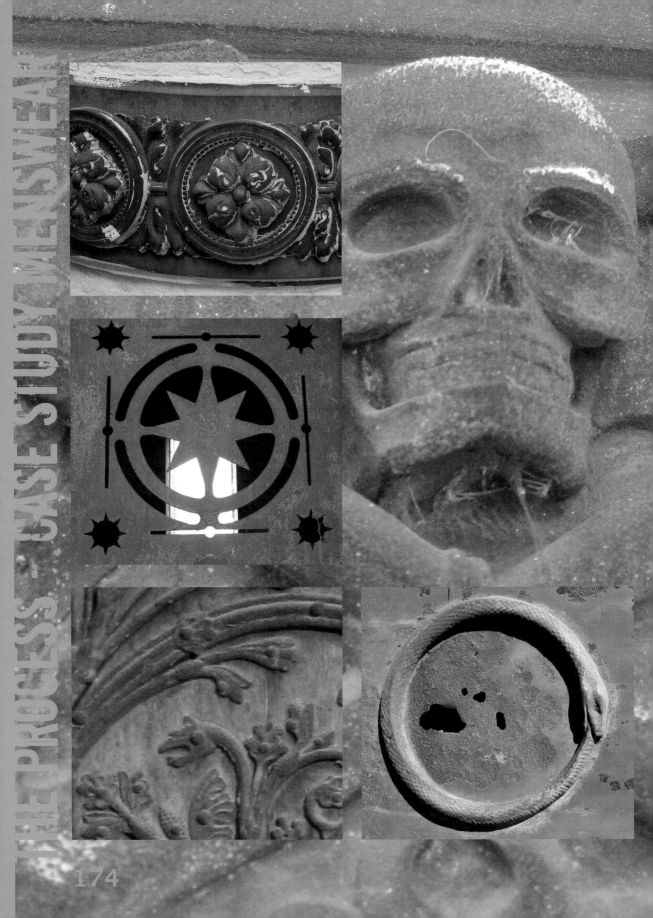

Kook

THEME & COLOUR

International Design Exchange Ltd.

FABRIC & SILHOUETTE

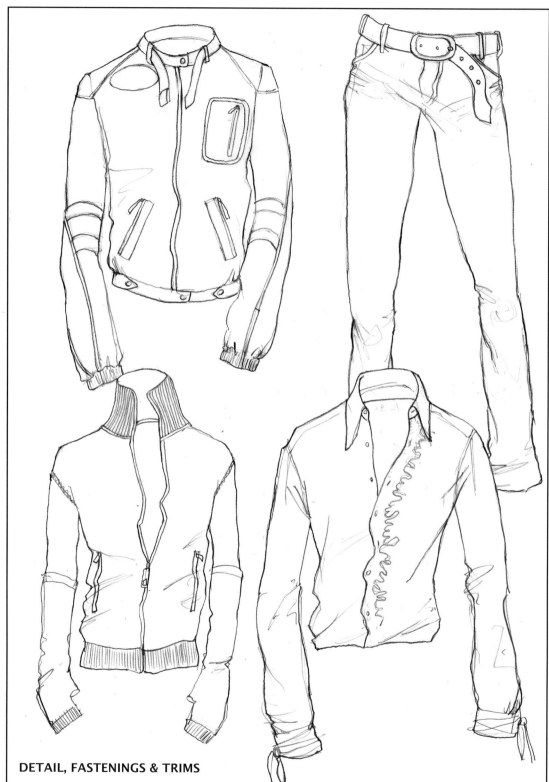

DETAIL, FASTENINGS & TRIMS

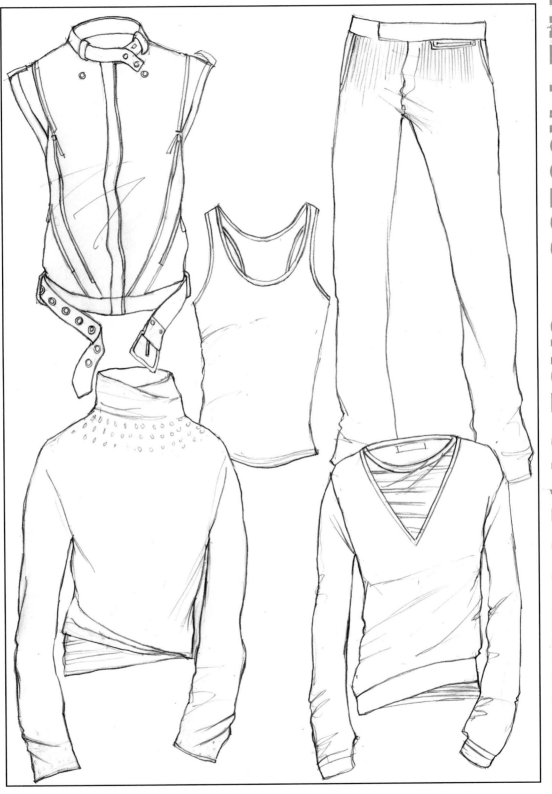

No : 456 8893 5544

nu-starr

poet

stock no 69 990ytrfrd/890 45

week 1 36

BRAND & GRAPHICS

PRODUITS EXOTIQUES

busker

THEME & COLOUR

FABRIC & SILHOUETTE

185

DETAIL, FASTENINGS & TRIMS

serial no 38765/98720/34/2
wash no 908-98708766570-1

KAYO

OFF SPRING

END GAME

BRAND & GRAPHICS

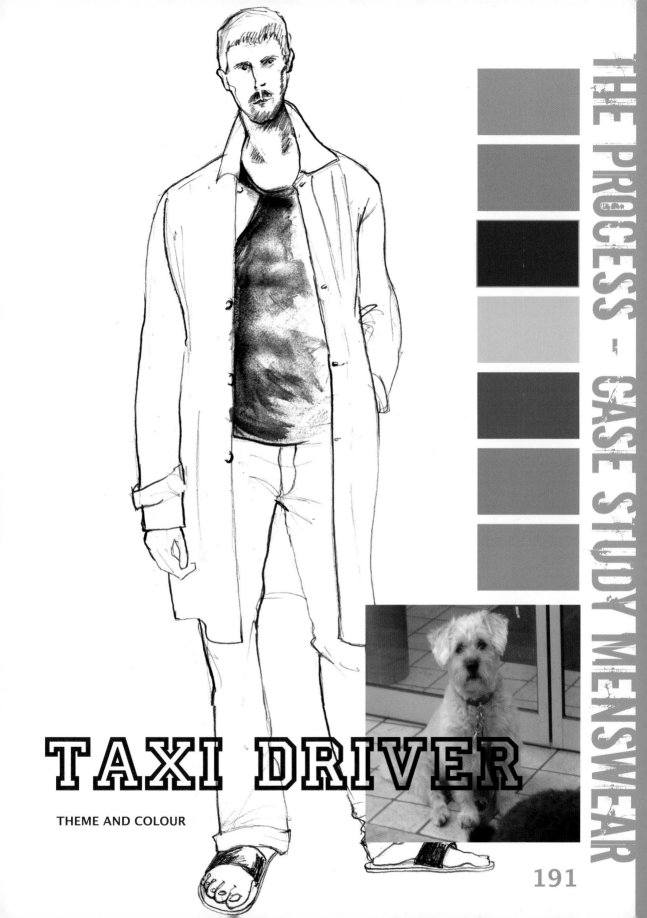

TAXI DRIVER

THEME AND COLOUR

FABRIC & SILHOUETTE

193

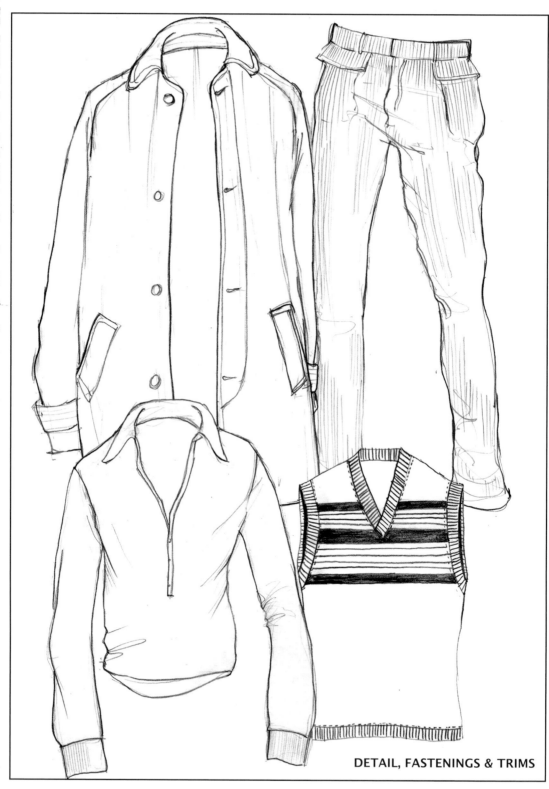

DETAIL, FASTENINGS & TRIMS

perryman

ISBN 0-224-03714-5

9 780224 037143

RED

BRAND & GRAPHICS

197

Fashion and graphics cross over in this section and fashion utilises the graphic language for communication.
The first part is about using typography and layout to communicate fashion forecasting information and mood. Examples of work then illustrate and communicate in a number of ways, through branding, packaging, limited edition publication and online via a website. In all cases, the information needs to be organised to communicate clearly.

It is not possible to fully inform about type and layout within the confines of this book, but some supporting rules of engagement and differentiation between classifying type may help. Further, more in-depth reading is available in the Bibliography.

The graphic designer uses 'grids' to organise and prepare layouts. A grid helps to create visual harmony and consistency throughout a multipage document and some tips are offered here.
'Desk Top Publishing' software, such as Adobe InDesign and QuarkXpress, now allow any designer to publish their work, in a professional manner, using grids and type, but without some basic grounding design problems may occur. This type of publishing software requires the designer to prepare imagery, such as, photographs – bitmap images – in Adobe Photoshop and illustrations – vector drawing – in Adobe Illustrator, before starting the layout as these are 'linked up' during designing. Some tips on how to use these pieces of software are available in Illustrating Fashion, by the authors, published by Wiley-Blackwell in 2007.
A basic tutorial in the use of Adobe InDesign is available in this section.

RIGHT – A RANGE OF FONTS FROM LUCIDA TO PALATINO – TEXT FONTS, FROM DOWNCOME TO STENCIL – DISPLAY FONTS

Order>Disorder
Lucida Grande 18pt

Order>Disorder
Helvetica 18pt

Order>Disorder
Arial 18pt

Order>Disorder
News Gothic 18pt

Order>Disorder
Bell Gothic Std. 18pt

Order>Disorder
Courier (TT). 18pt

Order>Disorder
Times 18pt

ORDER>DISORDER
Trajan Pro 18pt

Order>Disorder
Palatino 18pt

ORDER>DISORDER
Downcome 18pt

ORDER>DISORDER
Dirty Ego 18pt

Order>Disorder
Big Ruckus 18pt

ORDER>DISORDER
Nasty 18pt

ORDER>DISORDER
Nightmare 18pt

ORDER>DISORDER
Rosewood Std. 18pt

Order Disorder
Schism AOE. 18pt

ORDER>DISORDER
Transponder AOE. 18pt

ORDER>DISORDER
Stencil Std 18pt

Order>Disorder
Chicken Scratch 18pt

Order>Disorder
Bell Gothic Std. 18pt

Order>Disorder
Porcelain 18pt

♪rD.S.♪r>D.C.♪rD.S.♪r
Sonata 18pt

Skull Bearer AOE. 18pt

Linus Face AOE 18pt

Carta 18pt

ABOVE – DISPLAY FONTS AND PICTORIAL FONTS

There are a number of ways to classify font use: there is the serif (dynamic, angled and flowing) and sans serif (static and upright) approach, over simplified here. There is the 'point' size approach (the actual size of the font) and the sub-division of type into 'text' and 'display' fonts.
Text type tends to be used for continuous 'body' text use, the imparting of the content/information. Display type tends to be used in headings, sub-headings and titles to draw attention to an article or visual.

Digital fonts are accessible to all with a computer and there are many fonts available, to buy or download free from a number of websites, try www.1001freefonts.com or www.dafont.com.

There are calligraphic type fonts, distressed fonts and pictorial fonts.

Handmade type is also popular and should not be overlooked, when designing, to convey a particular mood.

LEFT – A SCRIBBLED FONT, STENCILLED FONT, BELOW – HAND DRAWN, PAINTED AND INVERTED

ORDER·DISORDER

ORDER=DISORDER

199

ORDER>DISORDER

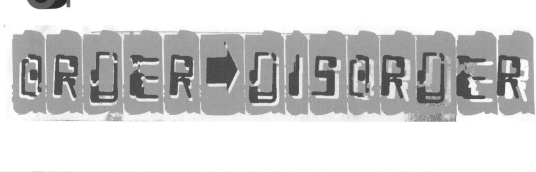

Type is the symbolic representation of words in its mechanical or digital form. Type is also about individual letterforms, systematically applied across characters into words, then into lines, then blocks of text.

Type can be expressive in its look, it can convey more than its content and there are 'fashions' in type as well as clothing. Type has been inspired by futurism, constructivism, Dadaism, and modernism; new attitudes to social cultural and political life emerged in the twentieth century and type became their visible artefact.

Scissors and glue assemblages of sentence fragments, taken from their original contexts, and then rearranged to create totally new meanings epitomise these type of developments. William Burroughs observed that "a word is not the object it represents; and the typeface takes one set of words and, through random acts, creates secondary levels of meaning".

Objects have been used to construct typographic language also.

Some type development has been borrowed from postmodernist theory and includes fragmentation, hybridity, parody, pastiche, wit and play. Postmodernism argued for the bringing together of 'ideas and forms from different times and places'. It also questioned history as continuous linear narrative.

Designers and artists to review should include, Kurt Schwitters, Cranbrook Academy, April Greiman, David Carson, Jamie Reid, Stefan Sagmeister, Neville Brody and Jonathan Barnbrook.

The typographic designer needs to understand the links between craftsmanship, historical understanding, cultural and technological issues, aesthetics and function, language and meaning.

SIMPLE TYPOGRAPHIC RULES

• For the best 'text' legibility choose classical typefaces, such as, Helvetica, Frutiger, Gill Sans, Univers, Times New Roman.
• Don't use too many different typefaces at any one time.
• Avoid combining typefaces that are similar in appearance.
• Text set in all capitals/upper case is hard to read. Use a combination of upper and lower case.
• For text type use point sizes that are most readable: 8pt to 12pt (dependent upon context).
• Don't use too many varying type sizes and weights at the same time.
• Avoid using over heavy or light typefaces for text – think Regular.
• Use typefaces that appear neither too wide or too narrow for text type.
• Use consistent letter and word spacing to produce an uninterrupted texture for text type.
• Lines that are too long or too short disrupt the reading process.
• For text type, use line spacing that carries the eye from one line to the next.
• For the best readability, use a 'flush left' 'ragged right' arrangement.
• Clearly indicate paragraphs – use indents or line spaces.
• Emphasise elements within the text without disturbing the reading flow.
• Don't arbitrarily stretch letters.
• Align letters and words on the baseline.
• If working with colour and type, make sure there is sufficient contrast between the background and the type.
• Break every rule with style and knowledge.

OPPOSITE – FROM TOP – TWO STENCIL FONTS MISALIGNED, FONT WITH 3D EFFECT APPLIED IN ADOBE ILLUSTRATOR, FONT CAPRICORN 38 – SOLID AND INVERTED VERSIONS SUPERIMPOSED, FONT WITH STROKES APPLIED TO CREATE 'DRIP' EFFECT IN ILLUSTRATOR, LETTER STAMPS WITH BLACK INK, CUT-UPS REARRANGED

201

HANDWRITTEN, PAINTED

HANDWRITTEN

CARVED, RAISED, SCRATCHY

HANDWRITTEN, PAINTED, FOUND OBJECT

CALLIGRAPHIC

TRADITIONAL

HAND PAINTED

ETCHED

EVERYDAY HANDWRITING SHOPS & SIGNS

Graffiti becomes a legitimate form of typography, it brings with it anti-establishment attitudes that defy conventional typographic rules and principles. It is more about 'style' rather than substance, as any suggested aggression is removed.
Sticker art and branding becomes an addition to signs and changes the meaning, often with humour.

STENCILS & TEXT BLOCK
ARRANGEMENTS

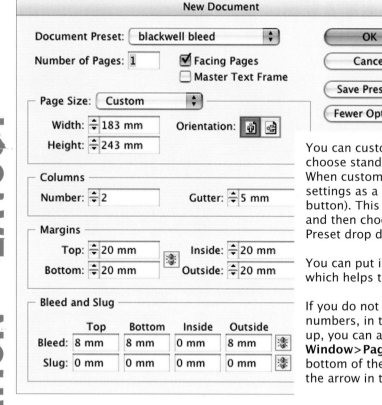

You can customise the page set-up or choose standard page sizes like A4. When customising you can save the settings as a Preset (under the Cancel button). This allows you to name it and then choose it from the Document Preset drop down field.

You can put in a number of columns which helps to organise a 'grid' system.

If you do not add enough page numbers, in the initial document set-up, you can add them by going to **Window>Pages** and then click on the bottom of the palette, or by clicking on the arrow in the top left-hand corner.

Adobe InDesign is a multipage layout programme that allows the designer to create books and documents.

It is very similar in interface design to Adobe PhotoShop and Illustrator which are complementary pieces of software that allow image editing and creation.

To create type in the software you do the following:
Open InDesign, go to **File>New Document** or **Book**, insert the number of pages required and all of the measurements needed. This example is the set-up for this book, portrait orientation, facing pages (to work in spreads) two columns with a 5mm gutter, 20mm margins and a 'bleed' of 8mm on each side except the bound edge, for images that bleed out over the edge of the paper for cropping purposes by the Printer.

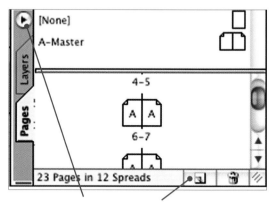

CLICK HERE TO ADD NEW PAGES

To add base grids (they help to align images and text) go to **View>Show Document Grid/Show Baseline Grid,** and/or **Show Guides. View>Show Rulers** is also helpful. Guides may be positioned by dragging from the top and side where the rulers are located to any position you require for alignment.

InDesign File Edit Layout Type Object Table View Window Help

SELECTION TOOL

TYPE TOOL

RECTANGLE FRAME

RECTANGLE FRAME TOOL

FILL

STROKE

APPLY NONE

LINKED IMAGE

THE TOOLBAR

THE MENU BAR

To link images click on the **Rectangle Frame Tool**, then draw a rectangle on the page, keep it selected (so that the tiny boxes at the corners are still visible), if it is not selected use the **Selection Tool**. Then go to **File>Place**, where you can choose the image you want to link into your layout.

You can create text in a similar way, create a rectangle, keep selected, then select the **Type Tool** and double click in the new rectangle, this will convert it to a Text Box, then write.

To manipulate the text go to **Window>Type & Tables>Character** or use the Menu Bar (top) to select the font and size.
If you click on the top drop down field, in the **Character Palette** below, you will be able to select a font; it allows you to choose the weight of the font e.g. Regular, Bold or Italicised and the Point size. Then you can manipulate the Kerning, Leading, Tracking, Baseline Shift etc. if this is display text.

Transform Paragraph ⇕ Character

FONT ——— Times

WEIGHT ——— Regular

FONT SIZE ——— 12 pt   (14.4 pt) ——— LEADING

KERNING ——— Metrics   0 ——— TRACKING

VERTICAL SCALE ——— 100%   100% ——— HORIZONTAL SCALE

BASELINE SHIFT ——— 0 pt   0° ——— SKEW

Language: English: UK

THE CHARACTER PALETTE

207

HOW THE CHARACTER PALETTE WORKS

The **CONTROL** Font
24pt size Lucida Grande

order>disorder

KERNING

o rd er>dis o r d er

VERTICAL SCALE

order>disorder

LEADING

order>disorder

TRACKING

order>d i s o r d e r

HORIZONTAL SCALE

order>disorder

SKEW

order>disorder

KERNING – This is the adjustment of space between characters. Place the cursor after the character to kern it.

VERTICAL SCALE – Stretches or contracts, vertically, the characters together.

LEADING – The spacing between lines of type.

TRACKING – The adjustment between selected characters.

HORIZONTAL SCALE – Stretches or contracts, horizontally, the characters together.

SKEW – Is capable of a false Italic to the left or right.

BASELINE SHIFT – Characters rest on an imaginary line, this function shifts them incrementally from that line (not demonstrated).

USING COLOUR IN INDESIGN

To change the colour of text go to **Window>Swatches**, select the text then select a colour from the Swatch palette. If the text adopts an outline/stroke click on **Apply None** on the **Toolbar**.

To introduce a more sophisticated colour palette click on the **Add Colour** arrow (opposite page) and click on **New Color Swatch**, then adjust the sliders accordingly and click on **Add**, the colour will appear in the **Swatches Palette.**

It is possible to add Pantone Process colours through this palette also by clicking on the drop down menu. Most full colour print work should be CMYK not RGB which is better for screen based activity.

208

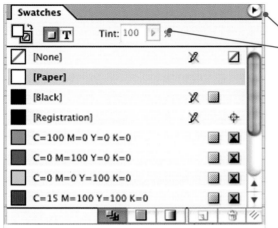

ADD COLOUR

CREATES TRANSPARENCY

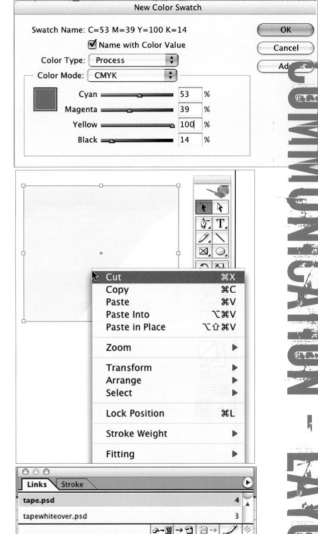

SWATCHES PALETTE

There are many useful tools in InDesign, some that operate in a similar way to Illustrator.

Shortcut access to useful tools can be achieved by clicking on the 'CTRL' key on a Macintosh computer, or right clicking on a PC; this produces menus, dependent on what is activated at the time. This allows the designer to economically select a function, for example, when **Placing** an image in a **Rectangle**, the CTRL menu can allow for the **Fit Content Proportionately** action.

When a document has been completed it is possible to create a PDF (Portable Document Format) that allows the document to be carried around and printed on any machine.

But, before you create the PDF you should do a check on the document, this is called Preflight. Go to **File>Preflight,** the computer will check the document to make sure everything works OK.

The Preflight will also alert you to any RGB files within the document giving you an opportunity to convert them. If you go to **Window>Links** and double click on each linked file, the dialogue box will explain whether the file is RGB or CMYK. Quit the dialogue box and go to the page with the offending file, click on it and use CTRL menu to select

Edit Original, this will take you to PhotoShop to edit the file, which will also automatically update in InDesign.

Once the Preflight check is perfect you can click on **Package**, which collects all images and fonts in one folder, from which you can create the PDF. Go to **File>Export**, name and select PDF and a destination. The PDF will be created.

209

Good layout design relies on a fundamental graphic concept: that of the GRID.

This is the unifying structure across a book or magazine. It helps to provide consistency and visual harmony to multipage or multiscreen documents. It helps to create structural hierarchies and coherence. The grid is useful for designing brochures, newsletters, flyers, web pages or books.

Grids allow the reader to navigate the printed page and in the case of magazines, allow for random access, so that content can be dipped into as the reader desires.
Grids are also useful where collaborations on larger projects require a number of people to input content.

However, it is not necessary, nor particularly aesthetically pleasing to use all of the grid elements all of the time.

Certain grids do raise particular problems, for example, narrower columns may result in more broken words, which has an effect on the readability. Sometimes 'rivers' may be formed where words may be hyphenated at the end of sentences. This is where the typographer may have to make design decisions.

It is possible to create numerous grids using Master pages in Desk Top Publishing software. In InDesign go to **Window>Pages**, then click on **A-Master** at the top of the page, create the layout on the selected page, then drag from the Master onto the main document to use that set-up. You can create as many Masters as you need.

For further reading on designing grids, refer to the Bibliography.

LEFT – SIMPLISTIC GRID DESIGNS

THE 'GLO' BRAND FABRIC STORY &
IDENTITY, ALL OF THE FOLLOWING
APPLICATIONS ARE BY RUTH
CAPSTICK

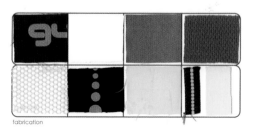

fabrication

GARMENT DESIGN & DETAILS, LAYOUT
FOLLOWS A SIMPLE GRID OF VISUALS
IN TOP TWO THIRDS, WRITTEN
INFORMATION BOTTOM THIRD

Firefly Jacket
PA Teflon Coated Ripstop
3M Reflective Polyester
Showerproof Nylon in 'Glo Yellow'
Hood With Draw String

Firefly Gilet
PA Teflon Coated Ripstop
3M Reflective Polyester panels and trim
Showerproof Nylon in 'Glo Yellow'
Front Chest Pocket

glo
Firefly Jacket/Gilet

211

MOOD ILLUSTRATION USING COLOUR STORY FOR CONTINUITY & STYLING SHOOT

On Two Wheels, a series of photographs taken whilst on a ride, played at different speeds with the effect of a digital flip book.

THE 'GLO' BRAND APPLIED TO CD-ROMS AND THEIR PACKAGING

212

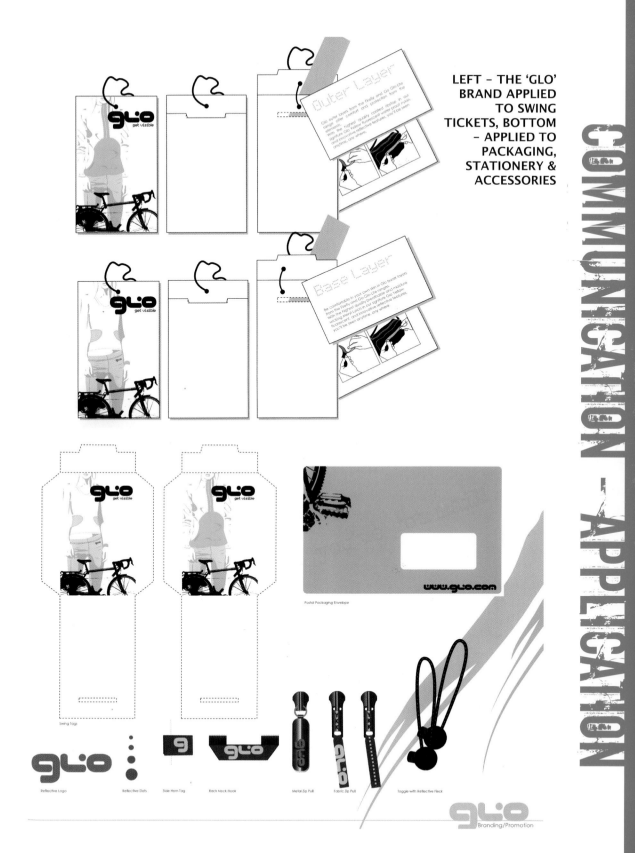

LEFT – THE 'GLO' BRAND APPLIED TO SWING TICKETS, BOTTOM – APPLIED TO PACKAGING, STATIONERY & ACCESSORIES

Outer Layer

Glo outer layers from the Firefly and Go Glo-Lite range offer comfort and protection in our elements. The highest quality coated ripstop in our signature Glo Yellow fluorescent water proof nylon, and innovative reflective features, you'll be seen anytime, any where.

Base Layer

Be comfortable in your own skin in Glo base layers from the Firefly and Go Glo-Lite ranges. With the highest quality breathable and moisture wicking Merril Urban out signature Glo Yellow, fluorescent and innovative reflective features, you'll be seen anytime, any where.

www.glo.com

Postal Packaging Envelope

Swing Tags

Reflective Logo   Reflective Dots   Side Hem Tag   Back Neck Hook   Metal Zip Pull   Fabric Zip Pull   Toggle with Reflective Fleck

glo
Branding/Promotion

213

**BRAND IDENTITY AND COLOUR STORY
APPLIED TO A WEBSITE DESIGN USING A
GRID OF HALF VISUAL, HALF TEXT BASED
INFORMATION**

Window   Help

Wed Aug 1st

Q▾ high visibilty

Q

ortswear for women,
ion and function

Hello...Welcome to glo.com

Come and see our fully functional and
rather fabulous range

With 10% Off Untill 14th August

simply click 'shop' then enter your exclusive password (available on
registration or on promotional leaflets at Glo sponsored events)

Go Glo Lite Jacket

Our most light-weight jacket with intregated high-visibilty featues will keep
you comfortable and safe whenever, wherever.

Plus tips on how to get the most out of our Go Glo Lite range.

Shop

Go Glo Lite Jacket   Glo Stuff   Brochure

glo

END NOTE

The greatest single factor to affect this industry has undoubtedly been the advent of global digital communication. This revolutionised practice and gave rise to new influential companies who were able to seize the potential of instant reportage to feed the insatiable appetite for 'new' within fashion. Some 15 years ago we initiated a research project intended to assess the impact of emerging digital technologies on the existing prediction industry which was, at that time, based on annual subscription to limited edition publications. We visited the offices of a small, new company, Worth Global Style Network who, along with a number of other emerging entrepreneurial companies, had grasped the potential of the Internet as a hub for multidisciplinary design exchange and broadcast. This company, now floated on the London Stock Exchange, has become a global corporation.

These web services, and the digital camera, have provided a new means for disseminating masses of information and business facts to executives and designers, enabling their decisions for forthcoming seasons to be based firmly on consumer preference. This multireportage and simultaneous global viewing has provided influence and inspiration between art, graphics, architecture and product design. It has been interesting to note that the advent of these large web based forecasting companies have not put the more traditional craft orientated publications and services, that were traditionally the bedrock of prediction, out of business. In fact these companies have survived to provide much needed specialist hands-on consultancy and to supply designers with publications and tactile colour pattern and texture samples.
The fashion cycle permeates all aspects of design to such an extent that products, fonts, graphics, even historical costume drama and film can all be easily pinpointed in time by their style. Trend forecasting has become a valuable means of analysing this cyclical process providing early intelligence about consumer needs and enabling companies to be effective and competitive. The term 'forecasting' is used less often now as newer terms are appropriated, for example: creative solutions, design intelligence, futures.

The most important observation of this book is that the systematic investigation into materials and sources, through research, is essential in the design process, providing inspiration, information and market intelligence. Information is available everywhere from newspapers, magazines and the Internet; it is consumed very rapidly, knowledge and information are important commodities, sometimes like disparate threads they need to be harnessed and organised to make sense of them.

Our investigation of contemporary forecasting aims to present a snapshot of contemporary working practice from the complex role of the fashion forecaster who seeks and edits information to the designer as interpreter and creator of products. This exploration of current forecasting practice illustrates the multidisciplinary nature of the industry, the diversity of trend forecasting agencies and the influence of evolving technologies and markets. We hope that this view into the world of design intelligence will inspire and inform the reader and acts as a useful resource on international contemporary practice.

"The future enters into us in order to transform itself in us long before it happens"

Rainer Maria Rilke
Letters to a Young Poet, August 12th 1904

END NOTE

BIBLIOGRAPHY
For further reading:

FASHION FORECASTING RELATED TEXTS
Brannon, E. (2000), Fashion Forecasting, Fairchild.

Craik, J. (1995), The Face of Fashion, Routledge.

Diane, T., & Cassidy, T., (2005), Colour Forecasting, Wiley-Blackwell.

Eundeok, K., & Fiore, A.M., (2001), Fashion Trends and Forecasting (Understanding Fashion), Berg Publishers Ltd.

Hines, T. & Bruce, M., (Eds) (2001), Fashion Marketing, Contemporary Issues, Butterworth-Heinemann.

Garfield, S., (2000), Mauve, Faber & Faber.

Perna, R., (1992), Fashion Forecasting, Fairchild Publications.

Seivewright, S., (2007), Basics Fashion: Research and Design, AVA Publishing.

Strauss, M. & Lynch, A. (2007), Changing Fashion: A Critical Introduction to Trend Analysis and Cultural Meaning, Berg Publishers.

TREND RELATED TEXTS
Evans, D., (2007), Coolhunting: A Guide to High Design and Innovation, Southbank Publishing.

Popcorn, F., (1996), Clicking: 16 Trends to Future Fit Your Life, Your Work and Your Business, Harper Collins.

Popcorn, F., & Marigold, L., (2001), Eveolution: The Eight Truths of Marketing to Women, Hyperion.

Rosen, E., (2000), The Anatomy of Buzz, Harper Collins.

Salzman, M., (2006), Next Now: Trends for the Future, Palgrave Macmillan.

BRANDING & TYPOGRAPHICALLY RELATED TEXTS
Gerber, A., (2004), All Messed Up: Unpredictable Graphics, Laurence King.

Jury, D., (2002), About Face: Reviving the Rules of Typography, Rotovision SA.

Klein, N., (2005), No Logo, Harper Perennial.

Monk, Jaybo, (2006), My Head is a Visual Township, Die Gestalten Verlag.

Mono, (2004), Branding: From Brief to Finished Solution, Rotovision.

Ries, A. & L. (2000), The Immutable Laws of Branding, Harper Collins Business.

Triggs, T., (2003), The Typographic Experiment: Radical Innovation in Contemporary Type Design, Thames & Hudson.

Wigan, M., (2006), Visual Thinking, AVA Publishing

PRODUCT RELATED TEXTS
Danziger, P., (2004), Why People Buy Things They Don't Need, Dearborn Trade Publishing.

Norman, D. A., (2005), Emotional Design: Why We love (or Hate) Everyday Things, Basic Books.

GRID RELATED TEXTS
Davis, G., (2007), The Designer's Toolkit: 500 Grids and Stylesheets, Chronicle Books LLC.

SOFTWARE SUPPORT TEXTS
Cohen, S., (October 2007), InDesign CS3 for Macintosh and Windows (Visual QuickStart Guide), Peachpit Press.

Weinmann, E., & Lourekas, P., (July 2007), Photoshop CS3 for Windows and Macintosh (Visual Quickstart Guide), Peachpit Press.

Weinmann, E., & Lourekas, P., (November 2007), Illustrator CS3 for Windows and Macintosh (Visual Quickstart Guide), Peachpit Press.

WEB
http://www.coolhunt.net
http://www.snapfashun.com
http://www.sachapasha.com
http://www.fashioninformation.com
http://www.zandlgroup.com
http://www.sheerluxe.com
http://www.stylingworld.com

BIBLIOGRAPHY

Company contact information in alphabetical order (this is not definitive, there are many agencies and services available in countries throughout the world, these are the ones that are better known in Europe, the United States and Australia).

Brandnewworld
231 West 29th Street
New York
New York
10001
USA
T: 212 967 5900
E: afeldenkris@brandnewworldus.com
W: www.brandnewworldus.com

Carlin International
79 Rue de Miromesnil
75008
Paris
France
T: +33 (0) 1 53 04 42 00
F: +33 (0) 1 53 04 42 08/10
Contact 'Style'
E: style@carlin-international.com
Contact 'Communication'
comm@carlin-international.com
W: www.carlin-groupe.com

Color Portfolio Inc.
USA
T: (866) 876 8884 tollfree
E: contact@colorportfolio.com

Concepts Paris
6 Rue Moufle
Paris
75011
France
T: +33 (0) 153 360608
E: www.concepts@conceptsparis.com
W: www.conceptsparis.com

Cotton Incorporated
6399 Weston Parkway
Cary
North Carolina
27513
USA
T: (919) 678 2220
F: (919) 678 2230

Faith Popcorn – Brainreserve
1 Dag Hammerskjold Plaza 16th Floor
New York
New York
10017
USA
T: 212 772 7778
F: 212 772 7787
W: www.faithpopcorn.com

Fashion Forecast Services
18 Little Oxford Street
Collingwood
VIC 3066
Australia
T: +61 3 9415 8116
F: +61 3 9415 8114
E: info@fashionforecastservices.com.au
W: www.fashionforecastservices.com.au

Fashion Snoops
60 West 38th Street
New York
New York
10018
USA
T: +1 (212) 768 8804
F: +1 (646) 365 6013
E: info@fashionsnoops.com
W: www.fashionsnoops.com

The Future Foundation
Cardinal Place
6th Floor
80 Victoria Street
London
SW1E 5JL
UK
T: +44 (0) 20 3042 4747
F: +44 (0) 20 3042 4750
E: office@futurefoundation.net
W: www.futurefoundation.net

Future Laboratory
Studio 2
181 Cannon Street Road
London
E1 2LX
UK
T: +44 (0) 207 791 2020
F: +44 (0) 207 791 2021
W: www.thefuturelaboratory.com

Henley Centre/HeadlightVision
6 More London Place
Tooley Street Place
London
SE1 2 QY
UK
T: +44 (0) 207 955 1800
F: +44 (0) 207 955 1900
E: betterfuture@hchlv.com
W: www.hchlv.com

Here & There
The Doneger Group
463 Seventh Avenue
New York
New York
10018
USA
T: 212 564 1266
W: www.doneger.com

Infomat Inc.
307 West 38th Street
Suite 1005
New York
New York
10018
USA
E: customercare@infomat.com
W: www.infomat.com

Jenkins Reports Ltd
44 Beckwith Road
London
SE24 9LG
UK
T: +44 (0) 207 733 0378
F: +44 (0) 207 737 1941
E: editorial@Jenkins-Reports.com
W: www.jenkinsreports.com

KM Associates
19 Heyford Road
Radlett
Herts
WD7 8PP
UK
T: +44(0) 1923 338205
F: +44(0) 1923 469509
E: mail@kmauk.com
W: www.kmauk.com

Milou Ket Styling & Design
Houttuinen 1
NL 1441 AG
Purmerend
The Netherlands
T: +31 299 433 638
F: +31 299 428 581
E: studio@milouket.com
W: www.milouket.com

Mode...information
Lisa Fielenbach
Heinz Kramer GmbH
Pilgerstraße 20
D-51491 Overath
T: +49 (0)2206 60 07 0
F: +49 (0)2206 60 07 17
E: info@modeinfo.com
W: www.modeinfo.com

Mode...information Ltd
First Floor Eastgate House
16-19 Eastcastle Street
London
W1W 8DA
UK
T: +44 207 4 36 01 33
F: +44 207 4 36 02 77
uksales@modeinfo.com

Mudpie Ltd
21-23 Home Farm Business Centre
Lockerly
Romsey
SO51 0JT
UK
T: +44 (0)1794 344040
F: +44 (0)1794 344056
W: www.mudpie.co.uk

Nelly Rodi
28 Avenue de St. Ouen
75018
Paris
France
T: 01 42 93 04 06
E: infos@nellyrodi.com
W: www.nellyrodi.com

Pantone, Inc.
590 Commerce Boulevard
Carlstadt
NJ 07072-3098
USA
T: 201 935 5500
F: 201 896 0242
W: www.pantone.com

Peclers Paris
Lucy Hailey
Holbrook Studio
Unit 12
53 Oldridge Road
London
SW12 8PP
UK
T: +44 (0) 208 675 8100
F: +44 (0) 208 673 3233
E: hh.peclers@mistral.co.uk
W: www.peclersparis.co.uk

Peclers Paris
23 Rue du Mail
75002
Paris
France
W: www.peclersparis.com

Promostyl
31 Rue de la Folie Mericourt
75011
Paris
France
T: +33 (0) 1 49 23 76 00
F: +33 (0) 1 43 38 22 59
W: www.promostyl.com

PSFK (trends) not mentioned in book
536 Broadway
11th floor
New York
New York
10012
USA
T: +1 917 595 2227
W: www.psfk.com

R.D. Franks – fashion books, trend, subscriptions and magazines
5 Winsley Street
London
W1W 8HG
UK
T: +44 (0) 207 636 1244
F: +44 (0) 207 436 4904
W: www.rdfranks.co.uk

Studio Edelkoort
30 Boulevard Saint Jacques
75014
Paris
France
T: 01 44 08 68 88
F: 01 43 31 77 91
E: studio@edelkoort.com

Stylelens
Head Office
8581 Santa Monica Boulevard
West Hollywood
CA 90069
USA
T: +1 310 360 0954
F: +1 310 659 9592
W: www.stylelens.com

Stylesight
130 West Third Street
Fifth Floor
New York
New York
USA
T: 212 675 8877
F: 212 675 8899
E: info@stylesight.com
W: www.stylesight.com

Trend Bible
Suite 1, Floor 2
Adamson House
65 Westgate Road
Newcastle upon Tyne
NE1 1SG
UK
T: +44 (0) 191 241 9939
F: +44 (0) 7734 694 014
E: enquiries@trend bible.co.uk
joanna@trendbible.co.uk

Trendstop Ltd
28–39 The Quadrant
135 Salusbury Road
London
NW6 6RJ
UK
T: +44 (0) 870 788 6888
F: +44 (0) 870 788 6886
E: contact@trendstop.com
W: www.trendstop.com

Trend Union
30 Boulevard Saint Jacques
75014
Paris
France
T: 01 44 08 68 80
F: 01 45 65 59 98
E: corinne@trendunion.com

Trendwatching.com
Laurierstraat 71–HS
1016 PJ Amsterdam
The Netherlands
T: +31 (0) 206 383 868
F: +31 (0) 206 389 498
E: info@trendwatching.com
W: www.trendwatching.com

View Publications
Martin Bührmann
Metropolitan Publishing BV
Saxen Weimarlaan 6
NL–1075 CA Amsterdam
The Netherlands
T: +31 (0)20 617 7624
F: +31 (0)20 617 9357
E: office@view-publications.com

WeAr Global Magazine
Klaus Vogel
Publisher & Editor
T: +43 6542 55106
F: +43 6542 551062
E: kv@wear-magazine.com
Subscriptions from:
Mode Information
Heinz Kramer GmbH
Pilgerstraße 20
D–51491 Overath
sales@modeinfo.com
W: www.wear-magazine.com

WGSN – Worth Global Style Network
Greater London House
Hampstead Road
London
NW1 7EJ
UK
T: +44 (0)20 7728 5773
F: +44 (0) 20 7785 8120
W: www.wgsn.com

Woolmark
Level 9
Wool House
369 Royal Parade
Parkville VIC 3052
Australia
T: +61 3 9341 9111
F: +61 3 9341 9273
W: www.wool.com

INDEX

INDEX

223